KV-585-714

WITHDRAWN
FROM
UNIVERSITY OF PLYMOUTH
LIBRARY SERVICES

# The Invisible Web: searching the hidden parts of the internet

## Paul Pedley

**Charles Seale-Hayne Library**
**University of Plymouth**
(01752) 588 588
LibraryandITenquiries@plymouth.ac.uk

Published by Aslib-IMI
Staple Hall
Stone House Court
London EC3A 7PB
Tel: +44 (0) 20 7903 0000
Fax: +44 (0) 20 7903 0011
Email: *aslib@aslib.com*
WWW: *http://www.aslib.com*

ISBN 0 85142 461 9 ✓

© Paul Pedley 2001

Except as otherwise permitted under the Copyright, Designs and Patents Act 1988, this publication may only be reproduced, stored or transmitted in any form or by any means, with the prior permission in writing of the publisher. Enquiries concerning reproduction outside these terms should be sent to Aslib at the address above.

The author asserts his moral right to be identified as such in accordance with the terms of the Copyright, Designs and Patents Act 1988.

UNIVERSITY OF PLYMOUTH

| | |
|---|---|
| Item No. | 9005694095 |
| Date | 1 1 NOV 2003 |
| Class No. | 025·04 PED |
| Cont. No. | ✓ |

PLYMOUTH LIBRARY

# The Invisible Web:
# Searching the hidden
# parts of the internet

Paul Pedley

# Is your organisation a corporate member of Aslib?

Aslib, The Association for Information Management, is a world class corporate membership organisation with over 2000 members in some 70 countries. Aslib actively promotes best practice in the management of information resources. It lobbies on all aspects of the management of, and legislation concerning, information at local, national and international levels.

Aslib provides consultancy and information services, professional development training, conferences, specialist recruitment, Internet products, and publishes primary and secondary journals, conference proceedings, directories and monographs.

Further information is available from:

Aslib-IMI
Staple Hall
Stone House Court
London EC3A 7PB
Tel: +44 (0) 20 7903 0000
Fax: +44 (0) 20 7903 0011
Email: *aslib@aslib.com*
WWW: *www.aslib.com*

# Contents

## 6. Selective list of invisible web

# List of abbreviations

| | |
|---|---|
| ACI | Autonomous Citation Indexing |
| ADAM | The Art, Design, Architecture & Media Information Gateway |
| ASP | Active Server Pages |
| BAILII | British and Irish Legal Information Institute |
| CGI | Common Gateway Interface |
| CML | Council of Mortgage Lenders |
| CORA | Computer Science Research Paper Search Engine |
| CORDIS | Community Research & Development Information Service |
| DETR | Department of the Environment, Transport and the Regions |
| DRM | Digital Rights Management |
| DSTP | Data Space Transfer Protocol |
| DVD | Digital Versatile Discs |
| EPO | European Patent Organisation |
| EU | European Union |
| FOLDOC | Free On-line Dictionary of Computing |
| FTP | File Transfer Protocol |
| HTML | Hypertext Markup Language |

| | |
|---|---|
| HTTP | Hypertext Transfer Protocol |
| IAR | Information Asset Register |
| IIS | Internet Information Server |
| IPL | Internet Public Library |
| ISAPI | Internet Server Application Programming Interface |
| ISO | International Standards Organization |
| ISP | Internet Service Provider |
| LII | Librarian's Index to the Internet |
| LLRX | Legal Library Resource Xchange |
| MIME | Multipurpose Internet Mail Extensions |
| MPEG | Moving Picture Experts Group |
| NECI | NEC Research Institute Inc |
| OECD | Organisation for Economic Co-operation and Development |
| OPAC | Online Public Access Catalogue |
| PDF | Portable Document Format |
| R&D | Research and Development |
| RAPIDUS | RAPId Delivery of Updates on Search Profiles |
| RECON | Regional Economic Conditions |
| SEC | Securities & Exchange Commission |
| TED | Tenders Electronics Daily |

| | |
|---|---|
| URL | Uniform Resource Locator |
| WYSIWYG | What You See Is What You Get |

# Series Editor

Sylvia Webb is a well-known consultant, author and lecturer in the information management field. Her first book, *Creating an Information Service*, now in its third edition, was published by Aslib and has sold in over forty countries. She has experience of working in both the public and private sectors, ranging from public libraries to national and international organisations. She has also been a lecturer at Ashridge Management College, specialising in management and interpersonal skills, which led to her second book, *Personal Development in Information Work*, also published by Aslib. She has served on a number of government advisory bodies and is past Chair of the former Information and Library Services Lead Body, now the Information Services National Training Organisation which develops National and Scottish Vocational Qualifications (NVQs and SVQs) for the LIS profession. She is actively involved in professional education and training and is also a former Vice-President of the Institute of Information Scientists. As well as being editor of this series, Sylvia Webb has written three of the Know How Guides: *Making a charge for library and information services*, *Preparing a guide to your library and information service* and *Knowledge management: linchpin of change*.

A complete listing of all titles in the series can be found at the back of this volume.

# About the author

Paul Pedley is Head of Research at the Economist Intelligence Unit. Prior to this Paul was Library & Information Services Manager at the law firm Theodore Goddard. Paul has also worked for the developers of Canary Wharf in London's docklands, and in government libraries at the Department of Trade and Industry, the Office of Telecommunications (OFTEL) and the Property Services Agency.

Paul is a Fellow of the Library Association, current chairperson of the Aslib Economics and Business Information Group (AEBIG), and he is a former chair of the Industrial and Commercial Libraries Group of the Library Association, the City Legal Information Group and the Property Information Group. He is a special libraries' representative on the Library Association Copyright Alliance.

Paul is the author of "Free business and industry information on the web", published by Aslib; as well as two Aslib Know How Guides – "Copyright for library and information service professionals" and "Intranets and push technology – creating an information sharing environment". He has also contributed to the 3rd edition of Aslib's "Copyright made easier", and to the "Handbook of information management" (formerly known as the "Handbook of special librarianship and information work"). Paul maintains his own website at http://www.paulpedley.com.

# Disclaimer

Whilst the author of this book has tried to ensure the accuracy of this publication, the publishers and the author cannot accept any liability for errors, omissions, or mistakes.

All of the URL's listed in this book were checked during February/March 2001 and were working at that time.

# Introduction

In a white paper published by BrightPlanet (2000) the "invisible" or "deep web" was said to be over 500 times larger than the "surface web", or the part of the web to which the search engines already provide access. It is a problem that many people are not aware of; and even if they have heard of the invisible web, they might not know just how extensive the problem really is. Indeed, the deep web is growing at a much faster rate than the visible or surface web and therefore the problem of not being able to search the internet effectively because of there being so many "deep web" sites is actually getting progressively worse.

Some people might argue that much of the invisible web isn't worth worrying about, that it contains all manner of ephemeral and useless information that simply isn't worth bothering with, and I have actually seen that point of view put forward in the professional press and also on internet discussion lists. It is certainly true that the deeper you go into the web, the more you will discover occurrences of duplication or spam. However, I think that the view that the invisible web is not worth bothering about is misguided because the reality is quite the opposite. Many of the resources that make up the invisible web are of a much higher quality than material that is found on the visible or open web. The BrightPlanet (2000) study found that total quality content of the deep web is at least 1,000

1

to 2,000 times greater than that of the surface web, and that the content is highly relevant to every information need, market and domain. A significant part of the invisible web resides in dynamic databases – those where you have to go directly to the site in order to undertake a search of the database. These sites generate a response to your query in the form of a web page which has been created "on-the-fly", and the page never existed in web page format until that moment. Dynamic databases often contain highly structured, professionally published content within a specific subject specialism and are therefore likely to retrieve much more relevant, good quality, high value results than anything you might get from searching one of the traditional search engines.

Amongst internet searchers there is undoubtedly a sense of frustration that it is not easy to undertake web searches which efficiently retrieve relevant, good quality results within a reasonable time frame.

A MORI research poll conducted on behalf of Mediapps revealed that 97% of internet users believe that it has lots of useful information. However, one in five of these users always feels that there might be something better on another site but do not know where to find it. With approximately 2 million new web pages appearing every day, internet users are finding it difficult to keep track of the best sources to find information that is relevant to them. The vast majority of internet users (77%) said that they found it to be the quickest way to access useful data. However, 64% waste a significant percentage of their time wading through irrelevant information and 42% find that it is often

2

difficult to find the information they are seeking (Aslib, 2000b).

A survey by Roper Starch Worldwide says that "a great majority (86 percent) of internet users feel that a more efficient way to search the web for accurate information should be in place" (Charny, 2000).

This frustration on the part of internet searchers is quite understandable, and I believe that the problems posed by the invisible web are a major contributor to the fact that web searchers cannot easily find what they are looking for on the internet, even though they might well have a gut feeling that there is something better on another site than the information that they have so far been able to find.

If a library user undertook a search on the library catalogue which failed to retrieve any records matching the topic of his or her search; and they subsequently found out that less than one per cent of the collection had been indexed on the OPAC they would be understandably outraged. And yet that situation is analogous to a web searcher undertaking an internet search using one of the traditional search engines, because a significant amount of data available via the web has not been indexed by the search engines.

This Know How Guide explores why the invisible web poses real problems for internet searchers, and what can be done to overcome those problems. The report contains an annotated list of search tools that can be used to explore the invisible web; a selective listing of some useful invisible web sites; and a number of worked examples showing how the invisible web can be used to answer enquiries.

# 1. What it is and how it works

In this chapter I want to try and define some of the concepts relating to the "invisible web". When people talk about the web they often use jargon and assume that the reader is bound to know to what they are referring. If an internet searcher has an understanding of the distinctions between the different parts of the web, then they will be aware of the limitations of web searching. This knowledge can be employed by internet searchers to good effect because that awareness then helps them to be able to undertake more focussed, and therefore more effective searches.

## Visible web

The visible web is the "publicly indexable" or "surface web" – those websites that have been picked up and indexed by the search engines.

## Invisible web

The phrase "the invisible web" refers to information that search engines can't or don't index. The content that resides in searchable databases, for example, cannot be indexed or queried by traditional search engines because the results are generated dynamically in response to a direct query.

Whilst the search engines might be able to index the home page of a database, they are unable to index each individual record within that database. So, in effect, an enormous amount of valuable content on the web is "invisible" because it is locked up within databases. BrightPlanet (2000) in its white paper about the invisible web avoided using the term "invisible web" because they considered it to be inaccurate, saying that the only thing "invisible" about searchable databases is that they are not indexable or searchable by conventional search engines. They identify the problem as being not a question of "visibility" or "invisibility" but the spidering technologies used by conventional search engines to gather their content. Instead of using the term "the invisible web" they use the phrase **"the deep web"** because whilst the information is somewhat hidden, it is still available if a different technology is employed to access it. The invisible web has also been referred to as **black holes in cyberspace**.

## Almost visible web

Search engines might only index a fraction of the number of pages that are available on a website. For example, with a website containing 200 pages, the search engines might have only indexed the first 50 pages. So, the remaining 150 pages might be largely hidden. It might well be that even though a page has not been indexed, it can still be reached indirectly because there could well be a link to it from one of the pages that the search engines have indexed. The reason for search engines imposing a limit on the number of individual pages to be indexed on a website is because of the sheer size of the web. The world wide web is so big that to index every single page available would put a great strain on the available computer power, and consequently the search engines may impose a limit on the number of pages that they retrieve from a web site. Strictly speaking, the unretrieved pages cannot be said to be part of the invisible web. Rather they are part of what might be referred to as the **"barely visible web"**, **"the opaque web"** or the "almost visible" web. The search engines have made a policy decision not to retrieve them by imposing a limit on the number of pages that they index from a specific site. If you find the site using a search engine, you will be able to go deeper into the site using hyperlinks on one of the web pages that has been indexed; or possibly from the site map of that particular website.

There are several key reasons why the opaque or barely visible web exists. These are:

- depth of crawl – the search engines may have a fixed limit on how many pages they will index within a site

- frequency of updating – whilst some sites are updated many times a day, the search engines might only revisit the site every few weeks or months and so there will always be a time lag between new data being loaded onto a site and the search engines indexing that new information. The search engines are not geared up for sites with real-time or frequently updated content

- robots.txt or the NOINDEX metatag – search engines use "robots" in order to scan and index a website. It is possible to tell them which pages and directories they can index by using the robots.txt file. However, some ISP's might not let you have access to the robots.txt file, in which case you can use the NOINDEX and the NOFOLLOW metatags. A value of "NOINDEX" allows the subsidiary links to be explored, even though the page is not indexed. A value of "NOFOLLOW" allows the page to be indexed, but no links from the page are explored.

## Vanishing web

Every day, thousands of websites disappear or become redundant. If you maintain a set of bookmarks or look after a site containing links to external websites, you will be very conscious of just how quickly some of your bookmarks or links become out of date. There are many reasons for this. It could be that the site has changed address; or that the site owner lost interest in maintaining the site; the company might have gone out of business or been taken over by another company; or the website could even have been forcibly removed from the web.

Even where the website is from a well known organisation, the page that you find most useful may no longer be there even if you are able to get to the home page of the site. To stay fresh, websites are often overhauled, revamped or re-launched. The webmaster might have changed the directory structure of the web pages on his/her site, resulting in the web page that you found particularly useful now having a totally new URL; or it may have been removed completely.

In the UK the British Library is the national deposit library, and publishers are required to deposit copies of UK publications with the British Library, and the other copyright deposit libraries. Now that so much information is "published" on the internet, indeed in some cases exclusively on the internet, there are real concerns that part of our cultural heritage is not being adequately protected for future generations. Websites come and go, they get updated and changed on a regular basis. What steps are being taken to create an electronic archive of these resources?

Re: source - The Council for Museums, Archives and Libraries (2000), in its response to the UK's Department for Culture, Media and Sport's five-year review of the British Library (BL), identifies the legal deposit of digital material as an 'urgent priority' for the BL if it is to retain its position as the national deposit library in the 21st century and beyond. Re: source praises the BL's efforts to tackle digital deposit within its voluntary code of practice, but suggests this is only a partial solution and expresses disappointment that provision for statutory digital deposit has not been made.

Some countries do have measures in place to try and preserve a snapshot of websites with the top level country domain code for their country. In Sweden, for example, the Royal Library makes a complete snapshot of accessible homepages every four months (Dupont, 1999).

## URL checking tools

I have already mentioned that hyperlinks to web pages need to be constantly monitored, otherwise an increasing percentage of them become broken links. There is even a word for this phenomenon – namely "linkrot". Rather than having to manually check each of your links individually on a regular basis, there are a number of tools available which do this for you automatically. Examples include:

- LinkGuard (http://www.linkguard.com)
- NetMechanic (http://www.netmechanic.com)
- Xenu's Link Sleuth (http://home.snafu.de/tilman/xenulink.html)
- Softgauge (for importing bookmarks from IE5 and checking URL validity http://www.softgauge.com)
- Link Scan's Quickcheck http://malch.elsop.com/quick.cgi

The Learning Resources department of the University of Northumbria at Newcastle has a web page about linkcheckers and site maintenance tools at http://www.unn.ac.uk/central/isd/links.htm

One way around the problem of entire web sites vanishing would be to save a copy of the website to your own computer. When you make a web page available offline, you can read its content when your computer is not connected to the

Internet. You can specify how much content you want available, such as just a page or a page and all its links. There are several ways that you can save the web page, from just saving the text to saving all of the images and text needed to display that page as it appears on the web.

## Saving pages with Microsoft Internet Explorer

If you are using the Internet Explorer web browser:

1.  On the File menu, click Save As.

2.  Double-click the folder you want to save the page in.

3.  In the File name box, type a name for the page.

4.  In the Save as type box, select a file type.

5.  Then select one of the following:

    *   **Web Page, complete** to save all of the files needed to display this page, including graphics, frames, and style sheets. This option saves each file in its original format.

    *   **Web Archive** to save all of the information needed to display this page in a single MIME-encoded file

    *   **Web Page, HTML only** to save just the current HTML page without the graphics, sounds or other files.

    *   **Text only** to save just the text from the current web page.

If you just want to save a picture, then right click on the image and choose Save Picture As. It is also worth considering whether to save a site's "Contact us" and/or "About us" pages so that even if the page does vanish, you have still got a note of their contact details.

## Saving a page in Netscape

To save an entire page:

Choose Save As from the File menu.

When you view a page containing frames and a frame is currently selected, the File menu's Save Frame As option is offered in addition to Save As. This lets you save only the page within the selected frame.

## Accessing pages that have disappeared

If you need to access a website which has disappeared, then there are a number of options available to you:

(a)    "climbing the tree" – this is the process of deleting the last bits of a web address until you find a stem page which still works. As an example, the Federal Reserve Bank of New York's publication "Current issues in economics and finance" can be found at http://www.ny.frb.org/rmaghome/curr_iss/2001.html. If for some reason you found that the page no longer worked, you could try working back step by step until you – hopefully – reach a page that could be accessed:

- http://www.ny.frb.org/rmaghome/ curr_iss/
- http://www.ny.frb.org/rmaghome/
- http://www.ny.frb.org/

(b) http://www.archive.org - the world's largest archive of websites. Founded in 1996 and located in the Presidio of San Francisco, the Internet Archive is a public nonprofit organisation that was founded to build an "internet library" with the purpose of offering free access to historical digital collections for researchers, historians and scholars. The collection includes:

a. World Wide Web pages (from October 1996 onwards, with no material that is less than six months old)

b. FTP sites (July to October 1996)

c. Usenet bulletin boards (October 1996 to late 1998)

Access to the collection is provided free of charge to researchers, historians and scholars. To gain access, enquirers need to complete a form proposing a project (http://www.archive.org/proposal.html)

(c) check if it is stored in Google's cache. Google takes a snapshot of each page examined as it crawls the web and caches these as a backup in case the original page is unavailable. If you click on the "Cached" link, you will see the web page as it looked when it was in-

dexed. The cached content is the content that Google used to judge whether this page would be a good match for your query. When the cached page is displayed, it will have a header at the top which serves as a reminder that this is a cached version of the page and not the page itself. Terms that match your query are highlighted on the cached version to make it easier for you to find out why the page is relevant to your search. The "Cached" link will be missing for sites whose owners have asked Google to remove the cached content. In a results list, at the bottom of each entry should be something along the lines of :
http://www.xyz.com/ - 5k – Cached – Similar Pages

In "Researching Online for Dummies" the web is divided up into three categories – the open web, the gated web, and the professional web (Basch & Bates, 2000)

## Open web

The open web consists of those web sites that are accessible to anyone via the search engines. They do not require the completion of a registration process, they are available free of charge, and their contents are not held within databases that have to be searched in order for a set of results to be retrieved. Because the open web consists of pages that the search engine spiders are able to crawl around, they can be retrieved via the search engines. One exception to that would be sites where the webmaster has specified that the search engine spiders should not index the site. Web site administrators can indicate which parts of their site should not be visited by a robot, by providing a specially formatted file on their site with the name robots.txt (see page 7).

# Gated web

The gated web consists of those websites which require identification before the user can enter the site. This may be a simple case of requiring the user to complete a free registration process; and then, next time they access the site they are required to enter their username and password. To make things easier, they might save these as a cookie, so that in future the username and password will automatically come up on the screen, and the user will just need to click on "OK". But there are also a number of web sites which are only available to paying customers, whether it be for a fixed subscription fee, or where you are charged on a pay per view basis.

# Professional web

The professional web refers to high-powered online services accessible through the web such as Reuters Business Briefing (http://www.business.reuters.com), Dialog (http://www.dialogweb.com) and Lexis-Nexis (http://www.lexis-nexis.com/professional). The professional web can normally be distinguished from the gated web by the search functionality available. The online services that form the professional web tend to have more sources, more search functionality, and more output options than the gated web.

# 2. The extent of the problem

When I hear someone say that they have searched the internet, I wonder whether they realise quite how much or how little of the total resources of the internet they have actually searched. How widely they have searched the sites available on the open web depends upon the search engine or other search tools that they have used. It is not possible to search the whole of the internet using one search engine, nor even one of the meta-search engines. Each search engine has only indexed a fraction of the content of the web, and whilst there is a certain amount of overlap between different search engines, there are also a lot of web pages that have been indexed by one search engine and not by another. One reason for this is the fact that the internet is growing dramatically every day, and it is difficult for search engines to keep up with the rapid growth in size of the internet.

Just how big is the internet? The internet is so dynamic that to try and put a figure on the size of the internet is in many ways a meaningless exercise, since any statistics would only relate to a particular snapshot in time. Things move on so quickly, and the search engines are all constantly trying to improve their coverage. There are a couple of excellent sources for information about search engines and how big they are. Greg Notess's website

(http://www.notess.com/search/stats/
sizeest.shtml/) is a good source for search engine
statistics. In October 2000, according to Greg
Notess's search engine statistics, the biggest search
engines (in decreasing order of size) were:-

1.  All the Web (FAST)
    http://www.alltheweb.com

2.  Google
    http://www.google.com

3.  Northern Light
    http://www.northernlight.com

4.  iWon (Advanced Search)
    http://www.iwon.com

5.  AltaVista
    http://www.altavista.com

Danny Sullivan's Search Engine Watch is also a
useful resource for information about search engines. In November 2000 there was an item on the
site about search engine sizes (http://
www.searchenginewatch.com/reports/sizes/
html) in which the top 5 [in terms of millions of
web pages indexed] was given as:

1.  Google!
    http://www.google.com

2.  FAST
    http://www.alltheweb.com

3.  WebTop.com
    http://www.webtop.com

4.  Inktomi
    http://www.inktomi.com

5.    AltaVista
      http://www.altavista.com

It is remarkable just how quickly the internet grows in size. In January 2000, for example, a study by search engine provider Inktomi (2000) and the NEC Research Institute showed that there were more than a billion documents on the web. But by July 2000, Cyveillance (2000) , a Washington DC area internet company had revealed that 2.1 billion unique publicly available pages exist on the internet according to their study "Sizing the internet" which also found that the internet is growing at an explosive rate of more than 7 million pages each day, indicating that it would double in size by early 2001. Then in October 2000 professors Hal Varian and Peter Lyman of the UC Berkeley School of Information Management & Systems (SIMS) reported that the directly accessible "surface" web consists of about 2.5 billion documents and is growing at a rate of 7.3 million pages per day (Maclay, 2000).

However, there is another problem, and it is one of which many people seem to be unaware. And that is the fact that there are many resources which, whilst they are posted on the web, are for one reason or another not accessible through the search engines. These resources are collectively known as the "invisible web". So, even if there was one search engine that had indexed the open web in its entirety, that would still leave the problem of how to retrieve material on the invisible web. A significant part of the invisible web consists of databases which use scripted programming such as CGI (Common Gateway Interface). These dynamic databases contain material that can only be found by going directly into the database in order to search the its contents. Each time you search the database, a set of results is generated "on the fly". That is, the search results are inserted into a web page template on demand. The results are generated as a one-off response to a query and vanish once the search has been completed. The reason that dynamic databases work in this way is that it is a manageable way of administering a resource that is constantly having new records added. If you go back a week or two later and perform the same search that you had undertaken only a few weeks earlier, you may well find that this time there are a few more results than you had retrieved the first time around. Some invisible web sites contain millions of documents within a dynamic database. It would be out of the question to manually create each database record as a web page, to assign each of these pages its own URL and to then link to each of those pages from other pages within the site.

Search engines tend to rely on technology that is designed to manage "static" pages as opposed to the "dynamic" information stored in databases. These static pages are generally known as "flat HTML" pages which have normally been generated manually using WYSIWYG web authoring tools. The problem is that companies now tend to create dynamic sites rather than static web pages. Consequently the invisible web is growing at a faster pace than the visible web.

Library catalogues are one example of dynamic databases. If you want to borrow a copy of a particular publication and want to know which library has a copy of that title in its collection, it is possible to do this on the internet. It does, however, mean having to sign into the catalogue of one specific library and do a search there; and then if you don't find the title that you are looking for, having to then move on and try the catalogues of another library. There is a listing compiled by Sheila and Robert Harden noting public libraries who make their catalogues available for searching via the internet at http://dspace.dial.pipex.com/town/square/ ac940/weblibs.html, while the British Library's public catalogue is available at http://blpc.bl.uk. Some library services might provide a union catalogue, but there may be instances where you would like to search across several catalogues from a number of disparate organisations that do not work together to create a union catalogue of their holdings. Some software packages make use of Z39.50 which enables users to search a number of catalogues simultaneously. However, to use this technology you need to know a number of things about each of the sites that you wish to search, and it can take time to fill in the technical settings for each of the library catalogues that you wish to access. So this is not a practical solution for people wishing to undertake *ad hoc* searches of lots of different catalogues very occasionally. The effort required in setting up such a facility can only really be justified if you make extensive use of certain library catalogues. Indeed, you would normally need the permission of the libraries concerned before gaining access to their data, and you may well be required to pay a fee in order to be able to access the full bibliographic records.

If you enter a search statement into a search engine it is possible to save the URL of your search, and what you are doing in effect is saving the search strategy, not a fixed set of results. This means that you can use this facility of saving the URL of your search as a means of current awareness. Whilst this may work for parts of the visible web, it is less likely to work on the invisible web. The problem with the invisible web is that most dynamically created web pages have changing and variable URL's, so it is not possible to rely on being able to save the URL as a means of saving the search.

Estimates of the size of the invisible web abound, and they vary considerably. I guess that it depends on quite what is being counted. On the one hand some people suggest that the traditional search engines have indexed around a quarter of the web, whereas BrightPlanet (2000) estimates that the invisible web is 500 times larger than the visible web.

According to BrightPlanet (2000), more than 95% of the information stored on the deep web is free. Indeed the actual figure they quote is 97.4% of the invisible web that is freely available without a priced subscription. In some cases it might be necessary to complete a registration form to access the information, even though the information itself remains free of charge. On their website http://www.completeplanet.com, BrightPlanet has listed 38,500 of the "content rich" databases that have been uncovered using their LexiBot software (see entry in chapter 5).

Search engines work by using automated programs known as spiders or robots in order to "crawl" the web. They then retrieve and index the pages that have been found. For spiders to locate web pages presupposes that there are hyperlinks to those pages. So, the reason why many web pages cannot be indexed is simply that there are no links pointing to a page that the spiders or robots can follow. As people become more aware of the contents of the invisible web they may mention them on a page on their website. If they post a dynamic URL address on a static web page, then it means that invisible web content will become discoverable by crawlers and therefore indexable by search engines. This is not, however, the same as saying that the entire contents of invisible web pages will be fully searchable via the search engines.

Some search engines work on the basis that results are ranked in order of how popular they are. This has the effect that those websites which are little-known, but which nevertheless contain some real nuggets, are overlooked. And a system of ranking results in order of popularity only exacerbates the problem of the invisible web, because it makes it even more likely that the least visited sites will continue to be overlooked. Some of the best information available on the web can be found on obscure web pages which are visited by only a handful of people each month.

Search engines are also more likely to index websites if lots of other people have created hyperlinks from their own website to those sites. Again, this makes it even more likely that "invisible web" sites will continue to be overlooked. Many of the search engines do have a facility which lets you see which websites have links to a particular URL. For example, in AltaVista you can enter the search: link:http://www.oecd.org to see who links to the OECD's website. The Linkage Reporter (http://www.searchengineworld.com/cgi-bin/linkage.cgi) on SearchEngineWorld has a facility to enter a URL and generate a report on how many links there are to a site. This checks a number of search engines such as AltaVista, Infoseek, HotBot, MSN, Lycos and Fast for link popularity. And it is possible to get a linkage report sent on a regular basis by email.

In a recent issue of the excellent *Tales from the terminal room*, Karen Blakeman (2001) noted five of the most irritating aspects of searching the web. These were:

- finding that the most promising looking page in your results list is inaccessible (you get an error 404 "file not found or 401/403 "Access forbidden" message)
- having to work out why a search engine has included your page in the results list when you cannot see any of your search terms in the page
- search pages cluttered with adverts and paid-for placements
- temperamental search engines that give you completely different results each time you run the search
- search engines returning pages and pages of irrelevant drivel.

Clearly the search engines have their limitations. Just as a good reference librarian would know their sources inside out, the pros and cons, the extensiveness of their coverage, their authoritativeness etc; so regular internet searchers would do well to build up a knowledge of the search tools available for exploring the web, and also develop a familiarity with a number of individual resources, some of which may form part of the invisible web. The challenge for the web searcher is keeping up to date with sources when sources come and go, or change at such a rapid rate.

# 3. What the invisible web contains

It can be hard to try and visualise just what it is that the invisible web consists of. It isn't just a black hole in cyberspace. Rather, its content is to be found in the following types of material:

| TYPES OF DATA | EXAMPLES |
| --- | --- |
| Medical databases | [Medline, for example, contains around 11 million references and abstracts] |
| Discussion lists | [such as BUSLIB-L] |
| Patent databases | [esp@cenet] |
| Phone numbers, e-mails, addresses etc | [BT PhoneNet UK, Yell – yellow pages] |
| Government databases | [Information Asset Register, UK Parliament Pages, which includes Hansard and Select Committee debates] |
| Scientific databases | [ResearchIndex] |
| Auction databases | [Internet Auction List, or eBay.com] |
| Legal databases | [BAILII] |
| Dictionaries, thesauri, etc | [xrefer] |

Product catalogues          [Amazon]

BrightPlanet (2000) found that the subject coverage of the "deep web" sites in their study were surprisingly wide ranging as follows:

| | |
|---|---|
| Humanities | 13.5% |
| News, Media | 12.2% |
| Computing/Web | 6.9% |
| Arts | 6.6% |
| Business | 5.9% |
| Health | 5.5% |
| People, Companies | 4.9% |
| References | 4.5% |
| Education | 4.3% |
| Employment | 4.1% |
| Lifestyles | 4.0% |
| Science, Math | 4.0% |
| Government | 3.9% |
| Law/Politics | 3.9% |
| Recreation, Sports | 3.5% |
| Travel | 3.4% |
| Shopping | 3.2% |
| Engineering | 3.1% |
| Agriculture | 2.7% |

BrightPlanet.com have put together a list of the 60 largest deep web sites at http://www.completeplanet.com/topsites/topsites_largest.asp These 60 sites contain data of about 750 terabytes, or roughly 40 times the size of the known surface web and it is estimated that they contain about 85 billion records or documents. BrightPlanet has also put together a listing of the most popular deep web sites at: http://www.completeplanet.com/topsites/topsites_mostpopular.asp

The types of information that would be part of the invisible web are described below.

## Databases requiring a log-in

A number of websites are password protected, requiring users to complete a registration process. In many cases the content is available free of charge, even though it is accessible only to registered users. Where sites have been password protected, the search engines are then unable to get beyond the log-in screen in order to index the site's content.

## Periodical archives

There are a number of useful periodical archives such as the magazine article search engine Magportal http://www.magportal.com and Findarticles.com http://www.findarticles.com which has an archive of published articles dating back to 1998 from more than 300 magazines and journals that can be searched for free.

## PDF documents

Until quite recently, search engines have ignored PDF files. However, Adobe Systems provide an Adobe PDF search engine http://searchpdf.adobe.com which has summaries for over a million documents on the web (see page 65).

More recently, Google have started to include listings of Adobe PDF files from across the web (see page 57). But at the time of writing it is still the case that most search engines have not indexed PDF documents.

# Dynamically generated data

Search engines and spiders cannot get inside dynamic databases. The only way to access the information is to search the databases themselves. This would include CGI scripts, javascript, or ASP. It is usually recognised by having a "?" in the URL, something that the search engines would normally treat as a truncation symbol and therefore be unable to index.

By their very nature, the dynamic databases available on the internet are going to be far more current and up to date than the information that is found on the "visible" web. They don't have to wait for a web page to be re-indexed, since they generate a set of search results on the fly, based upon the contents of the database at that moment in time. They generate dynamically created pages of results information which does not exist in web page format until you, the searcher, extract it from that database by entering your query to the web "front end".

# CGI scripts

When a user completes a form on the web, a CGI (or Common Gateway Interface) script or program is normally used to process that form when it is sent back to the web server. In effect CGI is a stand-ardised way for sending information between the server and the script. The CGI program does not communicate with the web browser directly. The browser talks with the server, the server talks with the CGI program, and the server talks back to the browser. It is CGI programs that work behind the scenes to process forms or look up records in a database. The CGI script then composes a response, normally as an HTML page. When it composes an HTML page, it is said to be generating HTML "on the fly". CGI scripts or programs are usually written using the programming language Perl, but they can also be written in other languages such as C++ or Visual Basic.

## Catalogues

One example would be Amazon.co.uk (http://www.amazon.co.uk) which has a searchable database of books, music, DVD's, videos, software and games. Another example would be library catalogues such as the British Library Public Catalogue (http://blpc.bl.uk).

## MacroMedia Flash

Flash is a Macromedia (http://www.macromedia.com) multimedia creator and plug in.

## Streaming media

"Streaming media" is content that contains audio, video and other media types. This is not normally captured by the search engines, and even if it were, the traditional search engines would not be very well suited to coping with the speed of updating that characterises streaming media web sites.

## Real time data

A lot of real time data such as share prices, weather, or airline/rail timetable information forms part of the invisible web. This is because of its ephemeral nature and also because it makes intensive use of computer storage.

## Knowledge bases

The invisible web contains a number of knowledge bases such as the Netscape Knowledge Base, Corel Knowledge Base, or Novell Support Connection Knowledge Base.

## Shop-bots

Consumers use search engines to locate and buy goods or to research decisions such as when they wish to select a holiday destination. Thanks to "shop-bots" they are now also making use of the many price comparison sites available on the web. These sites make it much quicker and easier than before to find out which supplier would be the cheapest for particular goods.

The shop-bot checks information from a number of sources, compares prices and reports back showing a list of shops and the prices they offer. It is, however, best to search more than one site and also to check whether the price that is shown is the total price. Does it, for example, include postage and packing. Whilst shop-bots sound like an excellent idea, they are only currently being used for very limited applications. They tend to cover a few key item types such as books, CDs, cameras, and computers; so it is not possible to get a quick price comparison of other goods. It would in any event be difficult to be able to compare prices on other items – would such a site be genuinely comparing like for like, or would it in some instances have to compare things that are supposedly equivalent substitutes?

Shop-bots on the web include:

| | |
|---|---|
| 2020Shops | http://www.2020shops.com |
| buy.co.uk | http://www.buy.co.uk |
| Checkaprice | http://www.checkaprice.com |
| Clickthebutton.com | http://www.clickthebutton.com |
| Dealtime | http://www.dealtime.co.uk |
| Kelkoo | http://uk.kelkoo.com |
| mytaxi.com | http://www.mytaxi.com |
| Priceline.com | http://www.priceline.com |
| Price offers | http://www.priceoffers.co.uk |
| Priceright | http://www.priceright.co.uk |
| Pricerunner | http://www.pricerunner.com |
| rusure.com | http://www.rusure.com |
| ShopSmart.com | http://uk.shopsmart.com |
| shoptour.co.uk | http://www.shoptour.co.uk |

# 4. The solution

## Awareness

The first step in solving any problem is to recognise that the problem exists. The invisible web represents a significant proportion of the overall contents of the web. Indeed, it is many times bigger than the visible or open web. Internet searchers need to be aware of the problem and the reasons why it exists in order to be able to develop effective search strategies which take account of the limitations of the traditional search engines. Hopefully raising the level of awareness will lead people to put pressure on the search engine companies to find ways around the problem; and for internet experts to examine ways in which the technology might be used to overcome existing problems. Webmasters need to be aware of the problems associated with dynamic databases and other invisible web resources. It is in their interests to drive as much traffic to their sites as they possibly can, and if they are able to make their web content more search engine friendly, they will be able to increase the amount of visits to their website(s). There are a number of solutions around for creating sites that the search engines are able to spider.

## Webmasters

So, what can webmasters do in order to get their sites indexed? Well, the traditional crawler-based search engines have problems indexing web pages delivered by dynamic databases for a number of reasons. One reason might be that they are unable to deal with certain symbols in the URLs generated by dynamic databases such as ?, &, %, $, or +. For example, the use of a symbol such as a question mark within an address such as http://www.xyz.com/cgi-bin/getpage.cgi?name=sitemap will cause most search engines to treat the "?" as a stop sign, and they will therefore treat the URL as being http://www.xyz.com/cgi-bin/getpage.cgi. As the URL is incomplete, this would mean that the user would get a "file not found" or 404 error message.

Another reason might be that the URL contains a reference to a CGI bin directory by using the string "cgi" or "cgi-bin" in the URL. The reason why this can cause problems is that the search engines want to avoid "spider traps" where the CGI process feeds it an infinite number of URL's, and as a result the spider gets stuck.

There are, however, a number of workarounds available that will enable webmasters to create URLs that the search engines can handle. The solutions are specific to the software that is used. Here are some solutions for a few of the more frequently used software packages.

## Active Server Pages

Microsoft's Active Server Pages (ASP) product is a server-side framework that lets users create web applications. The pages normally end with an .ASP file extension. Everything should be alright so long as the "?" symbol does not appear in the URL. However, if you are unable to avoid the use of the "?" symbol, then there are a number of products which are designed to make ASP sites more friendly to search engines.

One product is ASPSpiderBait which converts the PATH_INFO part of an HTTP header so that Microsoft's IIS (internet information server) sees the correct symbols but that for the purposes of web browsers (and search engine spiders), the characters are replaced in the URLs to something that is search-engine friendly:

? is replaced by _Q_
= is replaced by _E_
& is replaced by _A_

ASPSpiderBait is an ISAPI (Internet Server Application Programming Interface) developed plug-in that allows the use of parameter data in ASP pages which can be picked up by search engines. For further details see the website of the distributor http://www.webanalyst.com.au.

Another product is XQASP (http://www.xde.net) which also converts URLs of dynamic ASPs into a search-engine compatible format.

According to Paul Bruemmer active (2000) server pages have three major hurdles to overcome in order to get indexed by the search engines:

- convert dynamic ASPs into a search engine-compatible format or go off-site
- modify the HTML tags and content within the tags to gain high positioning

- submit all pages according to each engine's submission criteria.

The point concerning the need to submit pages according to each search engine's submission criteria is an important one, because each search engine has its own rules. Search engines often limit the number of submissions that can be made in a single day, and that limit will differ from one search engine to another. Multiple submissions could easily be considered by a search engine to be an attempt at spamming, and might lead to you being prevented from submitting web pages for registration with a search engine.

Where companies spend a lot of money on .ASP sites, then they obviously want to know that their investment has been worthwhile by ensuring that their site is visited as often as possible. Some companies modify pages for the purpose of search engine optimisation. These pages are known as "doorway pages", "gateway pages" or "splash pages". They could be a page within a website or an additional page – which is either added to the site, or hosted off-site.

Doorway pages are determined by the webserver that is running your site. When the webserver is asked by your browser for a URL such as http://www.xyz.com it responds by retrieving the "index" page. By default most webservers have as their default index.htm and index.html set up as the index page.

# Apache

The Apache web server software has a special "rewrite" module which translates URLs containing the "?" truncation symbol into a more search engine friendly format. Once installed, the rewrite module (or mod_rewrite) can translate a URL such as: http://www.catalog.co.uk/guide.html?cat=Food into the more search engine friendly http://www.catalog.co.uk/Food/index.html

For further information see http://httpd.apache.org/docs/mod/mod_rewrite.html and A users guide to URL Rewriting with the Apache Webserver by Ralf S. Engelschall http://www.engelschall.com/pw/apache/rewriteguide/

# Cold Fusion

Cold Fusion usually creates pages with the .cfm file extension, and there is normally a "?" symbol in the URL. Normally a URL would look something along the lines of http://www.xyz.com/page.cfm?ID=B105, but Cold Fusion can be reconfigured to generate URLs in the form http://www.xyz.com/page.cfm/B105.

Stepping back for a moment, it is worth asking whether you really need to generate pages dynamically at all. Often, the database is simply used as a page creation tool. If that is so, you might want to consider creating static pages instead, especially for sections of your site that don't change often. An alternative would be to create a mirror copy of your dynamic content into static pages which the search engines can spider. Tools that do this include:

eLuminator (http://www.mediadna.com/solutions.eluminator.html)

Xbuilder (http://www.xbuilder.com)

Position Pro (http://www.positionpro.com)

Inceptor (http:/www.inceptor.com)

I believe that the invisible web provides information professionals with a tremendous opportunity. It is undoubtedly the case that because many employees have access to the internet from their desktops at work, that they are able to answer a lot of their information needs using the web. Some have seen this trend towards disintermediation – having direct access to information sources without using an information intermediary – as a threat to the role of the information professional. But far from being a threat, the invisible web gives information professionals a great opportunity to demonstrate that they can add value to an organisation by developing an expert knowledge of the invisible web, and are therefore able to call upon a much wider range of web resources than most typical internet searchers. Information professionals need to ensure that they have a thorough knowledge of the resources that exist for their particular subject specialism; and that they have an understanding of the structure and limitations of web searching. That knowledge is something that comes only through the hard work involved in familiarising oneself with the resources available on the invisible web, and the tools that are available to make them known. And this knowledge, once acquired, needs to be kept constantly up to date especially in view of the speed with which things change on the web. In and of itself, the invisible web is certainly not a panacea. It is not the answer to all our problems. But in combination with a greater knowledge, awareness and understanding of web searching, information professionals can use the invisible web as part of the suite of information resources available to them for answering enquiries. This "search tool kit" or "search toolbox" relies upon the general search engines just as much as invisible web resources, and so the reader should not assume that I am trying to argue that only the invisible web is important.

# Netscape Navigator – what's related

The Netscape Navigator "What's Related" feature is part of the "Smart Browsing" facility on the Netscape browser. This facility provides the user with a list of URLs for web sites related to the page that you are currently viewing. Other facilities that are available within the "Smart Browsing" facility are:

• Internet Keywords: A shorthand way of typing addresses into the Location field

• NetWatch: A protection feature that lets you control the type of web pages that can be viewed on your computer.

To set up Smart Browsing:

1. From the Edit menu, choose Preferences.

2. Open the Navigator category and click Smart Browsing.

3. Select Enable "What's Related".

4. Select an option under "Automatically load 'What's Related' information." This option determines when Navigator fetches the related sites' URLs. The settings available are:

**Never:** Navigator waits until you click the What's Related button to fetch related sites' URLs.

**Always:** Navigator fetches the related sites' URLs automatically as soon as you visit a web page, whether or not you click the What's Related button.

**After first use:** Once you've clicked What's Related while visiting a page, Navigator fetches the information automatically whenever you return to that page.

5. List any domains for which you don't want related information. (This is optional)

6. Select "Enable Internet Keywords" if you want to type common words or brand names (instead of full URLs) in the Location field.

# Microsoft Internet Explorer's Show Related Links

If you just want to find web pages similar to the web page you are currently viewing, just click the "Tools" menu, and then click "Show Related Links".

# Reverse searching

One way to find "hidden" or covert websites would be to use reverse searching. This is the facility to find out who has linked to a particular site. For example, if you discover a good directory of invisible web search tools, you might want to do a reverse search on that directory. A reverse search of that kind could well yield all manner of useful sites covering the same topic.

SearchEngineWorld has a linkage calculator which automatically searches for links on half a dozen or so search engines. The facility is available at: http://www.searchengineworld.com/cgi-bin/linkage.cgi. In Altavista, for example, you can enter a search +link:www.xyz.co.uk in order to see which sites have hyperlinks directing users to http://www.xyz.co.uk.

Reverse linking is a facility that is used by web surfers to judge the authoritativeness and/or credibility of web sites. If a number of well known organisations are linking to a site, then it may well be considered by people as being a useful and reliable website.

The National Center for Data Mining at the University of Illinois at Chicago (2000) has launched a new infrastructure known as Data Space Transfer Protocol (DSTP) for creating the next generation of web data. This protocol is intended to standardise the way data is shared. "While there is a significant amount of data available online, it is stored in so many different formats that it has become difficult, if not impossible, to analyse and use in research" according to Georg Reinhart University of (2000). DSTP will enable researchers to search, analyse and mine databases simultaneously, even if the databases contain different types of data. The software is available at http://www.dataspaceweb. net (see also http://www.uic.edu).

According to Chris Sherman (2001a) "new web-centric query languages like WebSQL and new data format standards such as DSTP (Dataspace) have the ambitious goal of allowing searchers to query the entire web as if it were a single, unified database".

## Peer-to-Peer Computing

One of the most exciting developments has been the use of peer-to-peer computing. This is the technology used by companies such as Napster (http://www.napster.com), Pointera (http://www.pointera.com), and Gnutella (http://gnutella.wego.com). Whilst its best known use is as a means of sharing music files, it has much more potential than that. The technology enables direct searching of PC hard drives, and opens up new possibilities for internet searching. The direct linking and searching of PC to PC around the world to find information hidden away on other people's hard drives is incredible.

# 5. Directory of invisible web search tools

It may seem like an obvious question, but how can you search the invisible web if it really is "invisible"? Well, thankfully there are a number of resources that can help you to locate useful sources of information which are part of the invisible web. Typically, these resources do not allow you to undertake a full text search across the entire contents of the individual web sites. Instead they are often in the form of a portal or an index to invisible web resources. They might contain abstracts or descriptions of the material contained within those resources. These portals or indices are in some cases just browseable listings of resources arranged by subject or topic, whereas in other cases they may also provide the facility for users to search through all the abstracts and descriptions of the resources listed.

Unless you go directly into individual web sites containing dynamic databases or other invisible web resources, then it is helpful to find the gateways and directories that list invisible web sources. This chapter is a directory of invisible web search tools; while chapter 6 is a listing of a number of individual web sites with details of the sort of material they contain.

It is not possible to search the whole of the internet using one search engine. The traditional search engines only cover the open or visible web; and even then their coverage is incomplete. But when it comes to searching on what constitutes the invisible web, it is necessary to have a knowledge and familiarity of some of the individual websites that make up the invisible web and/or to utilise some of the indices and directories of invisible web resources.

A lot of the invisible web consists of dynamic databases. So, the first thing you need to know is which is the best source to go to for the topic that you are researching. And then you have to go directly onto that site in order to perform the search. This is analogous to searching nexis.com (http://www.nexis.com). The nexis.com service provides access to over 30,000 news, business and legal information sources containing around 2.8 billion searchable documents. These databases cover a wide range of different file formats such as free text databases, company directories, market research reports, numeric data or bibliographic information. Even the free text databases vary considerably in their formats. They may each contain a different set of fields or segments. Because the database formats vary so much, and also because of the fact that there are so many different databases, it is not possible to undertake a global search across the entire contents of all the databases available through Lexis Nexis. There are a number of file groups set up which allow cross file searching across a limited number of files, but a key factor in performing a successful and effective search on nexis.com depends upon choosing the right database to search at the outset. And that is also the case when searching the invisible web.

This chapter is a directory of some of the most useful resources for finding material on the invisible web. The sites listed act as pointers to useful websites, rather than providing full text searching across the invisible web.

**Name:**       All Seeing EYE investment meta-search engine

**URL:**        http://www.streeteye.com/cgi-bin/allseeing.cgi

**Provider:**   StreetEYE LLC.

**Description:** All Seeing EYE is a meta-search engine covering financial information. Users can search across a number of sites by entering a company name, ticker symbol, or search string; and they only need to enter this once in order to search across multiple sources. All Seeing EYE can also be personalised so that you are able to specify which are your favourite sources or services.

**Name:**       AlphaSearch (Calvin College – Hekman Digital Library)

**URL:**        http://www.calvin.edu/library/searreso/internet/as

**Provider:**   Calvin College

**Description:** AlphaSearch is a useful directory of "gateway" sites that collect and organize web sites that focus on a particular subject. For a site to be covered by AlphaSearch it must be accessible free of charge, and it must also be actively maintained. AlphaSearch contains over 800 records covering every discipline. Whilst 800+ records may not sound a lot, each site has been carefully selected because of its quality; and evaluated on the basis of its content, academic appropriateness and currency.

**Name:**      Beaucoup

**URL:**      http://www.beaucoup.com

**Provider:**      Teri Madden

**Description:**  Beaucoup contains an annotated listing of sites – primarily search sites – including directories, indices and search engines. The list covers over 2,500 sites, each of which contains free information. These sites can be browsed by subject; but users can also undertake searches on Beaucoup Super Search which is a meta-search tool powered by Mamma.com

**Name:**      British Library Public Catalogue

**URL:**      http://blpc.bl.uk/

**Provider:**      The British Library

**Description:**  The British Library Public Catalogue (BLPC) is a web interface to the main British Library Public Catalogues, offering both basic and advanced search options. It contains details of over 10 million books, journals, reports, conferences and music scores covering every aspect of human thought since 1450. The BLPC includes an additional music catalogue which heralds the first of many British Library files not previously available online.

**Name:**      BullsEye

**URL:**      http://www.intelliseek.com/prod/ bullseye.htm

**Provider:**  IntelliSeek Inc.

**Description:**  BullsEye Pro by Intelliseek is a desktop based meta search engine which can also access many of the sites covered by InvisibleWeb.com. BullsEye 2 refers to itself as being an intelligent desktop portal, and the software uses intelligent agents in order to be able to provide quick access to relevant information. It organizes over 800 search engines and databases into comprehensive search areas and categories to help you find exactly what you want in a few quick clicks.

Searchers can choose what kind of search they want to undertake:

- search the whole web
- find reviewed or selected web sites
- find web pages that link to a URL
- search for new web sites in the past week.

Since the web is a dynamic, constantly changing place, search engines often give results of pages that no longer exist or are irrelevant. Users can ask the BullsEye software to remove dead links from the results list and the software can also download and analyse web pages, removing results that are not relevant to your search. Search results can be saved as HTML reports which can either be e-mailed to others or saved for future reference. On first glance the software has a similar look and feel to Copernic (http://www.copernic.com), and as with Copernic users are required to download the software from the web. The free version of BullsEye does seem to offer quite a wide range of functions. For example, there is a facility to manage your internet bookmarks, regardless of whether they were generated in Internet Explorer or Netscape Navigator; and users can search their bookmarks by typing in part of the bookmark title or URL into the appropriate text box, and then clicking on the Find button. Power searching of your bookmarks is also possible either by entering multiple terms or using the Boolean AND/OR/NOT logical operators.

**Name:**        Citeline.com

**URL:**          http://www.citeline.com

**Provider:**    Citeline Inc.

**Description:** Citeline.com organizes web resources into categories that anticipate information needs in the healthcare industry. Users can enter their search terms on Citeline.com and they can specify whether they want to limit their search to sections for:

- disease and treatment
- news & journals
- organizations
- or research & trials.

There is a chargeable service, Citeline Professional, which allows users to search a number of additional categories:

- company information
- drugs/medical products
- medical economics
- discovery
- epidemiology
- regulatory.

CiteLine Professional provides access to systematically organized web sites, including hundreds of "invisible" web databases like the MEDLINE, NIH clinical trials, and US Patents databases. These databases contain some of the most valuable data on the web, but cannot be indexed by search engines. CiteLine Professional also includes a Site Monitor function for ongoing, automatic retrieval of new results from the Internet, and a Confidential Search capability that protects privacy.

**Name:**       Clip Art and Image Search

**URL:**        http://websearch.about.com/
                internet/websearch/
                msubmenu10.htm

**Provider:**   About.com Inc.

**Description:** The "Clip Art and Image Search" facility is part of the Web Search section on About.com maintained by Chris Sherman. This facility draws together resources for finding clipart, web graphics, multimedia, icons, paintings, photographs and other images on the web. There is an interactive image search wizard for searchers wishing to undertake a guided search of the available resources. There are listings of clip art search engines and directories for finding clip art, graphics, buttons and icons; fine art search resources covering online museums and art galleries, art education, artists, arts events, arts news and organisations; a listing of image search engines and directories for finding artwork, photographs and multimedia on the web; a multimedia search facility for locating multimedia files, including streaming video, MP3 (which is the most common format for transferring music files over the web), flash and other types of multimedia; and there is also a set of links for undertaking photography searches to find photographs and photography resources on the web.

**Name:** A collection of special search engines

**URL:** http://www.leidenuniv.nl/ub/biv/specials.htm

**Provider:** University of Leiden library

**Description:** There are a number of links to national or regional search engines, and general reference sources; but most of the links are discipline or subject specific, and are listed in alphabetical order of subject heading.

**Name:** Complete Planet

**URL:** http://www.completeplanet.com

**Provider:** BrightPlanet.com LLC.

**Description:** Complete Planet is a search engine and directory for the invisible web. The site has a keyword search facility, as well as a listing of around 38,500 "deep" web sites organised in twenty subject categories. Each category breaks down into numerous topical headings and listings for the individual sites include a description and rankings for relevance, popularity, and links (new sites are highlighted). The site also offers a detailed search tutorial and a white paper about the "deep" web (http://www.completeplanet.com/tutorials/deepweb/index.asp). CompletePlanet ultimately hope to list all deep web sites. The site also offers a detailed search tutorial and a white paper about the "deep" web.

49

**Name:**      ComputerSelect Web

**URL:**       http://www.computer-select.com

**Provider:**  Software Vista Inc.

**Description:** ComputerSelect Web provides IT information from a variety of sources such as trade and business journals, newsletters, newspapers, manufacturer's specification sheets and book publishers, product comparisons, company profiles, expert market research analysis, and pre-selected high-tech web sites. A list of the publications covered on ComputerSelect Web – currently around 200 - is available at http://www.computer-select.com/publist.htm.

The service is organised into sections:

*   Products – including product specifications, product reviews
*   Companies – Company profiles and articles about companies
*   Search all
*   Search the web
*   Glossary of computer and telecommunications terms

ComputerSelect Web taps the resources of the "invisible" web. With a single search, ComputerSelect Web users can gather the same information as if they had gone to many different web sites, which is especially efficient for dynamic-information searching - those queries you do over and over, such as stock prices. In order to be able to do this, ComputerSelect Web uses proprietary technology to search the full depth of pre-selected sites, returning specific results that an ordinary search engine would never be able to reach - let alone retrieve.

**Name:**     Copernic

**URL:**     http://www.copernic.com

**Provider:**     Copernic Technologies Inc.

**Description:** Copernic 2000 is an intelligent agent that carries out internet searches by simultaneously consulting the major search engines. To use Copernic requires the software to be downloaded from their website. The program has a number of key features:

- search results are scored and displayed according to their relevancy
- search terms are highlighted
- duplicate matches are removed
- searches can be updated and grouped into folders
- search results may be exported and/or emailed
- each search that you undertake can be saved
- you can specify that you wish the software to automatically update the search results for you.

**Name:**     Current Awareness Resources via Streaming Audio & Video

**URL:**     http://gwis2.circ.gwu.edu/ ~gprice/audio.htm

**Provider:**     Gary Price

**Description:** This is a compilation of links to audio/video services that can be used for monitoring current events. The links focus on news and public affairs services that are available in English.

**Name:** Direct Search

**URL:** http://gwis2.circ.gwu.edu/ ~gprice/direct.htm

**Provider:** Gary Price

**Description:** This is a compilation of links to the search interfaces of hidden web resources – those materials which are either not indexed by or only partially indexed by the traditional search engines. When I read articles about the invisible web, Gary Price's Direct Search seemed to be one of the most frequently mentioned sources for locating invisible web material.

**Name:** eLuminator

**URL:** http://www.mediadna.com

**Provider:** MediaDNA

**Description:** MediaDNA is a digital rights management (DRM) company. Their eMediator product is used to control digital content in order to protect valuable material; whilst eLuminator is a web promotion product aimed at driving traffic to your website. Search engines only have exposure to a small amount of content available on the web. The eLuminator product duplicates protected content in a way which makes it accessible to search engines without dropping any restrictions required for human visitors before they are allowed to view it. eLuminator is used on Inktomi.

**Name:** Fast Facts

**URL:** http://gwu.edu/~gprice/ handbook.htm

**Provider:**    Gary Price

**Description:** This reference compilation is a tool for finding fast facts such as those found in almanacs, factbooks, statistical reports or related reference tools.

**Name:**    Fossick.com – the Web Search Alliance Directory

**URL:**    http://www.fossick.com

**Provider:**    Leong Multimedia

**Description:** Fossick consists of a websearch alliance directory and a meta-search tool containing links to a collection of over 3,000 specialist search engines and topical guides. "Fossick" is an Australian and New Zealand word which means "to search for gold or gemstones, typically by picking over abandoned workings", and by extension, "to search, rummage or ferret out".

**Name:**    Gnutella

**URL:**    http://gnutella.wego.com

**Provider:**    Wego.com Inc.

**Description:** Gnutella's technology uses a distributed search model rather than the centralized approach used by most search engines. This means that when a distributed search engine tries to index pages, it is able to include invisible web data.

Gnutella is a fully-distributed information-sharing technology. When you run Gnutella client software and connect to the Gnutella Network, you bring with you the information that you wish to make public. The data that you have bothered to keep on your hard disk is what you found to be valuable. So when you share it you are sharing what is most valuable on the entire internet. And you control its sharing. That could be nothing, it could be one file, a directory, or your entire hard drive; although I would not advise users to make absolutely everything available for sharing, but rather to select key items that may be of interest to others.

Gnutella client software is basically a mini search engine and file serving system in one. When you search for something on the Gnutella Network, that search is transmitted to everyone in your Gnutella network "horizon" of 10,000 users. If anyone had anything matching your search, they will tell you.

Gnutella is not purely focused on trading MPEG music, it is a technology, a protocol MP3 or MPEG-1 audio layer 3 is a file format for music. It is a digital audio compression algorithm. Every client on GnutellaNet is also a server. There is a philosophy of give and take.

**Name:** Google (including Google PDF search)

**URL:** http://www.google.com

**Provider:** Google

**Description:** Google was ranked as the most popular search engine among business information users in the Business Information Resources Survey 2001 conducted by Gerry Smith on behalf of Headland Business Information which appears in the March 2001 issue of Business Information Review. It is also regarded as being one of the biggest search engines (see page 17). But I have included it in the listing of invisible web search tools because it has now started to include material that was previously considered to be "invisible" to the search engines. For example, Google now includes listings of Adobe PDF files from across the web. In order to restrict your Google search to just PDF files you can utilise the "inurl" feature. For example, "transport inurl:PDF" will retrieve documents that contain the word "transport" and which have "PDF" in their URL. This enables researchers to search for and retrieve some very useful sources of information via search engines for the first time including a number of reports from government departments, research reports, academic papers, reports and studies.

Google has also bought the usenet archive of Deja.com/Dejanews and made a large amount of their archives searchable again. The archive dates back to 1995 (Google 2001).

In December 2000 the Compass Internet Marketing Newsletter (http://www.visionmasters.com/newsletters/news_doc.htm) reported that "we have seen many of our client's. ASP pages of product database information get crawled by Google and ranked fairly well on very specific search terms", but they are unsure as to whether this will become a widespread practice.

**Name:**     HotSheet

**URL:**     http://www.hotsheet.com

**Provider:**     HotSheet.com Inc.

**Description:** HotSheet is an Internet website directory, or portal, which specialises in listing popular and useful web destinations. There are 12 primary categories which provide over 500 links to premier sites.

**Name:**       Infomine scholarly internet resource
                collections

**URL:**        http://infomine.ucr.edu/
                search.phtml

**Provider:**   Library of the University of California

**Description:** Infomine is a virtual library and reference tool which contains links to useful internet resources such as databases, electronic journals, electronic books, bulletin boards, listservs, online library card catalogues, articles and directories of researchers.

**Name:**       Internet Oracle Search Engines

**URL:**        http://www.internetoracle.com

**Provider:**   Internet Oracle Inc

**Description:** Search forms and direct links to hundreds of search engines from general purpose directories to niche topic indexes. Coverage includes search engines, meta searches, find people, find companies, maps, jobs, health & medical, women's resources, and travel.

**Name:**       Internet Public Library (IPL) Reference Center

**URL:**        http://www.ipl.org/ref

**Provider:**   University of Michigan School of Information

**Description:** The IPL is a virtual library that provides a good starting point for finding reference works, subject guides, and specialized databases.

**Name:**       Invisible Web.com

**URL:**        http://www.invisibleweb.com

**Provider:** IntelliSeek Inc.

**Description:** The InvisibleWeb Catalog contains over 10,000 databases and searchable sources that have been frequently overlooked by traditional search engines. Each source is analysed and described by editors to ensure that users can find reliable information on hundreds of topics. The service consists of a blend of proprietary technology and human editors. The technology checks the directory to clean up dead and duplicate links.

**Name:** The invisible web home page

**URL:** http://www3.dist214.k12.il.us/invisible/default.html

**Provider:** Ken Wiseman

**Description:** The "Invisible Web home page" site supports Ken Wiseman's presentation on the invisible web for educators (Wiseman, 1999). The site contains a presentation with slides on the invisible web; a resources section covering educational links that are not always indexed by web search tools; a link to Ken's article about the invisible web; and a searching section which suggests places to start an internet search, including data collections, reference, directories, publications, politics, and commerce

**Name:** Kenjin

**URL:** http://www.kenjin.com

**Provider:** Autonomy Systems Limited

**Description:** Kenjin examines the concepts, not the keywords, in your active window and delivers relevant links.

**Name:**      Lexibot

**URL:**        http://www.lexibot.com

**Provider:**   BrightPlanet.com LLC.

**Description:** Lexibot is a software package developed by BrightPlanet. Using the software, an internet searcher is able to enter a single search request that will simultaneously search both the visible web and parts of the invisible web – dynamic databases which can be accessed via the internet. Searches are not as quick as those undertaken on typical search engines, particularly more complex searches. The LexiBot automates the process of making dozens of direct queries simultaneously using multiple thread technology.

**Name:**      Librarian's Index to the Internet

**URL:**        http://lii.org/

**Provider:**   Berkeley Digital Library SunSITE

**Description:** A virtual library that is both searchable and browseable, this is an excellent source for specialized databases. It consists of an annotated directory of over 6,400 internet resources which have been evaluated and selected by librarians for their usefulness to the users of public libraries. Only the best resources are included. The advanced search facility on LII makes it possible to undertake very precise searches within the directory of resources.

**Name:**      The Library of Congress Online Catalog

**URL:**        http://catalog.loc.gov

**Provider:**   Library of Congress

**Description:** The catalog contains approximately 12 million records which are made up of records for books, serials, computer files, manuscripts, cartographic materials, music, sound recordings, and visual materials. The catalog can be browsed by subject, name, or call number; as well as being fully searchable.

**Name:**      LibrarySpot

**URL:**        http://www.libraryspot.com

**Provider:**   StartSpot Mediaworks Inc.

**Description:** LibrarySpot collects links to quality reference resources and provides links to libraries around the world. It is one of a family of vertical information portals. Others in the StartSpot family include GenealogySpot (http://www.genealogyspot. com); PeopleSpot (http://www.peoplespot.com); and GovSpot (http://www.govspot.com).

**Name:**      Lycos Directory > Reference > Searchable Databases

**URL:**        http://dir.lycos.com/Reference/ Searchable_Databases/

**Provider:**   Lycos Inc.

**Description:** This is a branded version of Intelliseek's invisibleweb.com database of databases, and Invisible Web Catalog results are seamlessly integrated into the Lycos search process. If you undertake a search on Lycos, watch out for any "hits" which have a "Searchable _Databases" link in the results.

**Name:**      Multimedia Search

**URL:**        http://websearch.about.com/ internet/websearch/msub42.htm

59

**Provider:**     About.com Inc.

**Description:**  The multimedia search facility is part of the web Search section on About.com maintained by Chris Sherman. It consists of a set of links to a number of specialist search facilities for locating multimedia files, including audio, video, MP3, and other streaming media.

**Name:**       News Center

**URL:**        http://gwis2.circ.gwu.edu/ ~gprice/newscenter.htm

**Provider:**     Gary Price

**Description:**  A huge directory of links to up to the minute news stories. The links relate to text-based news services including wire services, major newpapers and news weeklies, world news, and business publications. There are also links to sites that have facilities for searching current news.

**Name:**       Northern Light

**URL:**        http://www.northernlight.com

**Provider:**     Northern Light Technology Inc.

**Description:**  The Northern Light Special Collection is an online business library comprising 7100 full-text journals, books, magazines, newswires, and reference sources which are organized into custom search folders. The breadth of information available in the Special Collection is unique to Northern Light, and includes a wide range of diverse sources such as American Banker, ENR: Engineering News Record, The Lancet, PR Newswire, and ABC News Transcripts. This content is fully searchable integrated with the web, or on its own

through Power Search at http://www.
northernlight.com/power.html.

**Name:**        OneLook

**URL:**          http://www.onelook.com

**Provider:**   OneLook

**Description:** OneLook is a special search engine
that finds on-line dictionaries and glossaries containing the word you look for. The actual dictionaries are provided by other web sites.

**Name:**        People Finders and White Pages

**URL:**          http://websearch.about.com/
                  internet/websearch
                  msubmenu17.htm

**Provider:**   About.com Inc.

**Description:** People finders and people search engines help you find the address, telephone number
or email address of friends, family members and
celebrities. This facility is part of the Web Search
section on About.com maintained by Chris
Sherman.

**Name:**        Pointera

**URL:**          http://www.pointera.com

**Provider:**   Pointera

**Description:** The Pointera Sharing Engine was
designed primarily for portals and content sites; and
it lets users of those sites share legitimate files
through a standard web browser. For sites which
use Pointera, the Pointera Sharing Engine installs
automatically when a user visits the site, just like a
java chat client. Pointera's real-time indexing technology ensures that download links almost always

work because the links are updated every few seconds, unlike traditional search engines which may take several months to re-index the data.

The system is used to share files of all types from Microsoft Office documents, PDF documents and HTML files through to MP3s, video clips and images.

**Name:**   Price's List of Lists (Gary Price)

**URL:**   http://gwis2.circ.gwu.edu/ ~gprice/listof.htm

**Provider:**   Gary Price

**Description:**  Price's List of Lists is a clearinghouse for numerous lists of information found on the Internet. Many of these lists present information in the form of rankings of different people, organizations, companies, etc. Many too have been designed to be interactive or searchable, providing functionality that is only possible in electronic format. The list is an extremely useful resource. It draws together in one place hundreds of lists of information and organises them into subject headings. Whilst it is true that a number of these lists could be retrieved through the search engines, I think that the search engines would have trouble indexing some of the most useful links. Looking through the HTML source code for Price's List of Lists web page, I was struck by how many of the links contained references to cgi-bin, or the "?" symbol (see the discussion in chapter 4 of how search engines have problems indexing URLs containing cgi-bin, "?", etc).

**Name:**   ProFusion

**URL:** http://beta.profusion.com and http://www.profusion.com

**Provider:** Intelliseek Inc.

**Description:** ProFusion is a "deep web" search engine which searches over 1000 sources – invisible, opaque and visible. Profusion enables simultaneous searching of select popular sites like About.com, FAST, Britannica, MSN Search, Raging Search (AltaVista), and others; and directly searches over 500 invisible web sites, such as Adobe PDF, TerraServer, etc. Overall the number of results from ProFusion will be smaller than searching individual search engines because it is designed to give you a manageable number of highly relevant results rather than a large pool of irrelevant results. It is possible to increase the number of search results per engine beyond the default setting of 10. To undertake database searching you can also select the databases to be searched, rather than relying on the default settings.

**Name:** Public Record Office Online Catalogue

**URL:** http://catalogue.pro.gov.uk/ListInt/Default.asp

**Provider:** Public Record Office

**Description:** A database of around 8.5 million document references from the United Kingdom's Public Record Office. The information can be accessed either through searching or browsing the contents of the catalogue.

**Name:** Real-Time Tracking and Monitoring

**URL:**          http://websearch.about.com/
                  internet/websearch/
                  msubmenu18.htm

**Provider:**     About.com Inc.

**Description:** A collection of links to web sites for real-time quotes, to locate the current position of packages, satellites, airplanes, traffic and road conditions, and weather reports. This facility is part of the Web Search section of About.com which is maintained by Chris Sherman.

**Name:**         Refdesk.com

**URL:**          http://www.refdesk.com

**Provider:**     refdesk.com

**Description:** Redesk.com is a portal of links to reference sources.

**Name:**         Researcha

**URL:**          http://www.researcha.com

**Provider:**     Researcha

**Description:** The Researcha site, which was launched in October 2000, has a free reports section. This is a searchable database containing details of market research reports available on the web free of charge. In some instances it is necessary to complete a registration form on the site that has produced the research you want, but in many cases there is a link straight through to the document itself. The reports are rated with one, two, or three stars; three stars representing the most valuable material. Each record in the free reports database contains the title of the report, a brief description, the name of the organisation producing the research, the date of publication, the three star rating, document type (eg. PDF, html etc) and the file size. In addition to the facility to search across the database, there is also a listing of latest additions, and a complete listing of all the reports that have been given the full 3 stars for their rating. Whilst some of the material may be freely available on the web, it is certainly not easy to track down. The fact that most of the documents are in PDF format; or the need to complete a registration process to access some of the material; means that many of the research reports would not be easily retrieved by a standard search of the web.

**Name:**        The Scout Report

**URL:**         http://www.scout.cs.wisc.edu/report/sr/current/index.html

**Provider:**    Internet Scout Project

**Description:** The Scout Report is a good way to keep up with new search tools, especially specialized databases. You can view the weekly report and the archive of previous Scout Reports on the web. You can also have the report delivered to you via email by subscribing through a listserv. Send a message to listserv@cs.wisc.edu and type "subscribe SCOUT-REPORT" in the body of the message or got to http://scout.sc.wisc.edu/misc/lists/. There is a full-text search facility to search through the archive of over 10,500 Scout Report summaries.

**Name:**        Search Adobe PDF online

**URL:**         http://searchpdf.adobe.com/

**Provider:**    Adobe Systems Inc.

**Description:** Search engines normally ignore PDF files and list only content on HTML pages and text files. The Adobe PDF search engine has summaries for over a million documents on the web.

Entering a set of search terms, the user is then presented with a results list giving brief details about the documents retrieved. Selecting one of these does not take the user to the full PDF document immediately, but rather to an abstract or summary describing the document concerned. There is also a listing of the keywords that have been assigned to that document. If, having read the summary, you decide that the document is what you are looking for you can then go to the full document. Having this interim step is helpful because it saves the user from loading a memory-hungry file before they have been able to establish whether or not the document is of interest.

| | |
|---|---|
| **Name:** | Search engines, databases and newswires @ Internets |
| **URL:** | http://www.internets.com |
| **Provider:** | wwwINTERNETS Inc. |

**Description:** This site consists of a filtered collection of useful search engines and newswires. To find the most appropriate search engine for their search, users can either enter a concept in order to find a search engine that is relevant; or they can choose a subject heading from a drop-down menu. The links to on-line resources include news feeds, archives, libraries, research databases, catalogues, and statistical data.

| | |
|---|---|
| **Name:** | Search Engine Guide: the guide to search engines, portals and directories |
| **URL:** | http://www.searchengineguide.com |

**Provider:**   K. Clough Inc.

**Description:** The site has links to around 3,700 search engines. These have been arranged into 16 broad category headings, and can therefore be browsed by subject. In addition to the search engine links, industry experts have joined together to create a search engine and portal knowledge base. Articles and tutorials from the site's content partners provide insight into all aspects of the industry. Users of the site can also subscribe to a daily email newsletter of search engine, portal and directory news headlines.

**Name:**   Search Systems Public Record Databases

**URL:**   http://www.pac-info.com/index.shtml

**Provider:**   Pacific Information Resources Inc.

**Description:** A directory of around 2,400 links to free searchable public record databases which primarily covers North America, although there is a global section covering worldwide public records.

**Name:**   Searchability: guides to specialist search engines

**URL:**   http://www.searchability.com

**Provider:**   Paula Dragutsky

**Description:** The site consists of an annotated listing of guides to specialised search engines covering hundreds of subjects. The sites are listed in a number of different ways – there is a listing of giant guides, the largest guides with the most detailed subject categories; a guide focussing on popular topics; a guide to regional search engines and a guide to academic search categories.

**Name:** Special Search Engines

**URL:** http://www.ntu.edu.sg/library/ specialcat.htm

**Provider:** Nanyang Technological University Library

**Description:** This is a listing of specialist search engines which is organised by their geographic coverage or by specific subjects and topics. A number of the sites listed are dynamic databases, and can therefore be considered to be part of what constitutes the invisible web.

**Name:** Speech and Transcript Center

**URL:** http://gwis2.circ.gwu.edu/ ~gprice/speech.htm

**Provider:** Gary Price

**Description:** A huge directory of links to a wide range of recorded speeches and transcripts, from politicians, businessmen and other famous people. The site includes a collection of links to historic speeches.

**Name:** SpeechBot

**URL:** http://speechbot.research. compaq.com

**Provider:** Compaq Corporate Research

**Description:** An experimental streaming media search engine from Compaq. Speechbot is a search engine for audio and video content that is hosted and played from other websites covering areas such as current affairs, the Internet, or personal investment. Speechbot's speech recognition software, its indexing technology and its index-searching technology work together to make a large volume of audio material available on the web.

**Name:**      VerticalNet

**URL:**      http://www.verticalnet.com

**Provider:**      Vert Tech LLC.

**Description:** This site is primarily designed for E-commerce and provides links to specific "online communities" - a great resource for links to web information on different industries such as high tech, energy, food/packaging, science or manufacturing.

**Name:**      The Virtual Acquisition Shelf & News Desk

**URL:**      http://resourceshelf.blogspot.com

**Provider:**      Gary Price

**Description:** This site covers resources and news for information professionals and researchers. It is a weblog or "blog" with the basic concept of being an acquisition shelf specialising in quality web resources and news.

**Name:**      WebData.com

**URL:**      http://www.webdata.com/

**Provider:**      ExperTelligence Inc.

**Description:** WebData is a database portal which has links to thousands of databases, carefully classified and organized for rapid, easy access; and there is also a set of comparative shopping tools.

**Name:**      Webgator

**URL:**      http://www.webgator.org/

**Provider:** Dave Guss

**Description:** Webgator is a set of links to investigative resources on the web. The site is particularly useful for people information. Subject headings include topics such as adoption resources, cemeteries & obituaries, courts & court records, missing persons, property records, and sex offender registries.

**Name:** WEBnME.COM Web Search - Links

**URL:** http://www.webnme.com/search/index.html

**Provider:** WEBnME.COM

**Description:** Provides a set of links to useful resources, some of which are sites on the invisible web. The headings include:

- ask a question
- find business information
- find e-mail addresses
- find people
- find public records
- find telephone numbers
- web search engines

**Name:** YBLost.com

**URL:** http://proagency.tripod.com

**Provider:** YBLost.com

**Description:** A valuable collection of links to a variety of specialised search resources, particularly strong for public records, government information and people search tools.

**Name:**      Zapper

**URL:**       http://www.zapper.com

**Provider:**  Zapper Technologies Inc.

**Description:** Zapper lets you highlight blocks of text and submit them as search queries. "Zaplets" let you access a number of high-quality invisible web sites.

# 6. Selective list of invisible web resources

## Art & Architecture

**ADAM**, the Art, Design, Architecture & Media Information Gateway
http://adam.ac.uk/index.html is a searchable catalogue of over 2,500 internet resources.

**American Art Directory**
http://www.artstar.com/bin/aad_home. Database of 100,000 artists, artworks (including high resolution images), venues, and related websites.

## Books

**Amazon.co.uk**
http://www.amazon.co.uk. Search for books, music, DVDs and videos, software, PC & video games.

**Barnes & Noble.com**
http://shop.barnesandnoble.com/oopbooks/oopsearch,asp?userid=4CJQ002LNY&mscssid=&sourceid=&salesurl= rare, secondhand, and out of print book search.

**Bookfinder.com**
http://www.bookfinder.com/ search engine with a database of 20 million new, used, rare and out of print books.

**Internet Bookshop**
http://www.bookshop.co.uk. The Internet

Bookshop@WHSmithOnline was established in 1993 and has a database of 1.4 million English-language books in print.

**Waterstone's Online**
http://www.waterstones.co.uk has search and buy facilities for British Books in Print.

# British Politics/Government

**Information Asset Register**
http://www.hmso.gov.uk/inforoute/index.htm. Gateway to information held by UK government departments. The Information Asset Register (IAR) aims to cover the vast quantities of information held by government departments and agencies. This includes databases, old sets of files, recent electronic files, collections of statistics, and research.

**The Stationery Office**
http://www.the-stationery-office.com. Is a good starting point for information from The Stationery Office and across government. As well as the Stationery Office catalogue the site has links to other sites such as UK official publications on the internet and the London Gazette.

**UK parliament pages**
http://www.parliament.the-stationery-office.co.uk/cgi-bin/empower?DB=ukparl includes parliamentary publications such as select committee reports, the register of members' interests and the Weekly Information Bulletin. http://www.parliament.uk/commons/HSECOM.HTM

# Charities

## Register of Charities in England and Wales
http://www.charity-commission.gov.uk/cinprs/
first.asp. Contains details of all charities registered
in England and Wales – around 180,000.

# Company information

## BestCalls.com
http://www.bestcalls.com. Many public companies are providing their latest earnings releases via
a web conference call. This site, launched in 1999
operates a public directory of investor conference
calls.

## Business Credit USA (infoUSA)
http://www.businesscreditusa.com/. Database of
around 12 million companies which has free credit
ratings, plus access to more detailed priced credit
reports.

## Companies House
http://www.companies-house.gov.uk/.
Searchable database of UK registered companies
by company name or number, including the facility to search on dissolved names, previous names,
or proposed names.

## Crawfords directory of city connections online
http://www.crawfordsonline.co.uk. Crawford's
concentrates on the relationship between major UK
companies and their advisors. Coverage is not limited to quoted companies but includes private companies with an annual turnover greater than £15m.

# Computers & Internet

### Computer Science Research Paper Search Engine (CORA)

http://cora.whizbang.com/. Search engine providing access to 50,000+ research papers on all computer science subjects.

### ebusinessforum.com

http://www.ebusinessforum.com. Provides insight and analysis to help senior executives build strategies for doing business in the global digital economy including items on best practice within industry sectors, doing ebusiness in 60 countries, news stories, and interviews with key players in the industry.

**FOLDOC**: Free on-line dictionary of computing http://www.foldoc.org

### Nua Internet Surveys

http://www.nua.ie/surveys/. Source for internet demographics and trends

# Country information

**OECD international regulation database** http://www.oecd.org/subject/regdatabase/index.htm. Internationally-comparable set of information about the state of regulation and market structures in OECD countries.

**Prices and earnings around the globe** – UBS Swiss Economic Research http://www.ubs.com/e/index/about/research/pcc/publications.html

# Demographic Information

## International Database (U.S. Census)
http://www.census.gov/ipc/www/idbacc.html. The International Database (IDB) is a computerized data bank of statistical tables of demographic and socio-economic data for 227 countries and areas of the world.

**The World Gazetteer**: Current population figures for cities, towns and places of all countries. http://www.gazetteer.de/home.htm

# Economic Information

## Current value of old money
http://www.ex.ac.uk/~RDavies/arian/current/howmuch.html. Set of links to websites which can answer the question "how much would a specified amount of money at a certain point in time be worth today".

## Economagic
http://www.economagic.com/. Site for free economic time series data.

## EH.Net - how much is that?
http://www.eh.net/hmit answers questions concerning the comparative value covering purchasing power, interest rates and other variables between the past and today. The site includes a form for calculating the purchasing power of the dollar and the pound.

# Education

## Association of MBAs

http://www.mba.org.uk. The Association represents the interests of MBA students and graduates, leading business schools and MBA employers. The site includes a facility to search for an MBA programme http://www.studylink.com/mba.

## OECD Education Database

http://www.oecd.org/scripts/cde/viewdb.asp? and then select the "Education" heading. The OECD online education database provides internationally comparable data on key aspects of the education systems.

# European Information

## CORDIS

http://www.cordis.lu (Community Research & Development Information Service) is a source of information on EU R&D programmes. It helps companies to participate in EU funded research programmes by providing a searchable database of calls for proposals/tenders, and a database of companies seeking partners. There is also a facility for registered CORDIS users to create and save database search profiles which is called RAPIDUS – RAPId Delivery of Updates on Search profiles.

## Court of Justice, Luxembourg

http://europa.eu.int/cj/index.htm. The website gives access to recent case law of the Court of Justice and the Court of First Instance, including details of pending cases.

**EUR-Lex: European union law**
http://europa.eu.int/eur-lex/en/index.html is a
database of legislation in force in the European
Union covering:

- Treaties
- Official Journal – most recent issues from the
  past 45 days
- Legislation in force
- Consolidated legislation
- Community preparatory acts
- Case law.

**The legislative observatory**
http://wwwdb.europarl.eu.int/dors/oeil/en/
default.htm  is a database covering the activities of
the institutions involved in the legislative procedure
and decision-making process. Each procedure has
a file containing all documents relating to 3 stages:

- the pre-legislative stage, possibly in the form
  of a preparatory note supplying the context
  of the procedure;
- the progress of the procedure, from the initial proposal or vote in committee to the final
  act or opinion;
- the legislative follow-up, including a general
  evaluation of the procedure, the problems
  and the outcome.

**RAPID** (the Spokesman's service of the European
Commission)
http://europa.eu.int/en/comm/spp/rapid.html is
a database of press releases covering European
Commission, Council of Ministers, Court of Justice,

Court of Auditors, Economic and Social Committee and the Committee of the Regions.

**Tenders Electronics Daily (TED)**
http://ted.eur-op.eu.int/ojs/html/index2.htm is the Official Journal "S" series of tender documents.

# Exhibitions

**Exhibitornet.com**
http://www.exhibitornet.com/text/showsearch/index.htm. Exhibitor Magazine Group's online resource for trade show and event marketing professionals. Includes a database of forthcoming exhibitions.

# Finance *see* Investing/Finance

# Government *see* British Politics/ Government

# Health & Medical Information

**Medline**
www.nlm.nih.gov/databases/freemedl.html contains around 11 million references and abstracts.

**Medline Plus**
http://medlineplus.gov. Healthcare information, including consumer health information from the National Library of Medicine.

**National Electronic Library for Health**
http://www.nelh.nhs.uk/. The UK's National

Electronic Library for Health Programme is working with NHS Libraries to develop a digital library for NHS staff, patients and the public.

**NHS Direct** http://www.nhsdirect.nhs.uk/. Gateway to health information on the internet including a searchable section on conditions and treatment and an A-Z guide to the NHS.

# Historical Documents/Images

### Public Record Office
http://www.pro.gov.uk/releases/default.htm. This page has links to the images of a number of public records for 1970 which were released on 1 January 2001 (see also the entries for Public Records on page 88).

## Interactive Lists

### The Rich List 2000
http://www.games.newsint.co.uk/cgi-bin/richlist?-aSTART. The list is searchable by name, source of wealth, or by words appearing within the text of entries. The survey appeared in the Sunday Times newspaper for 19th January 2000. (See back issues at http://www.sunday-times.co.uk/news/pages/resources/library1.n.html).

# Investing/Finance

### Financial Times Company Info (Global)
http://www.globalarchive.ft.com/cb/cb%5Fsearch.htm

**IPO SuperSearch**
http://www.edgar%2donline.com/ipoexpress/
supersearch.asp. Searchable database of initial public offerings.

# Jobs

**Monster.co.uk**
http://www.monster.co.uk. Searchable database of UK, European and global jobs.

**Stepstone**
http://www.stepstone.co.uk. Career and recruitment portal with details of UK and European jobs.

# Journal articles

**findarticles.com**
http://www.findarticles.com is an online search service covering articles from over 300 journals and magazines. Searches can be undertaken across the entire database, or within subject categories; or articles can be browsed within subject headings or by name of magazine.

**Full-Text Sources on Dialog and DataStar**
http://library.dialog.com/fulltext/index.html.
Covers over 4,000 titles.

**Magportal**
http://www.magportal.com/ is a tool for finding magazine articles on the web. I have found this source to be particularly useful. I did a search on the phrase "invisible web" and retrieved an item by Bill Mickey (Mickey, 2000) which on further investigation does not include the phrase "invisible

web" within the text, and would not have been easy to find through the search engines.

**Publist**
http://www.publist.com is a publications directory covering over 150,000 magazines, journals, newsletters and other periodicals.

**Uncover periodical database**
http://uncweb.carl.org. UncoverWeb is a current awareness and document delivery service.

**United States Government Internet Periodicals (Under construction)**
http://198.252.9.108/home/govper.html. Provides access to full text internet government periodicals.

# Language/Translation Tools

**EuroDicAutom**
http://eurodic.ip.lu/cgi-bin/edicbin
EuroDicWWW.pl is the multilingual terminological database of the European Commission's translation service. It contains technical terms, abbreviations, acronyms and phraseology.

**Verbix Verb Conjugator**
http://www.verbix.com/index.html. Linguistic software that conjugates verbs in over 50 languages.

# Legal

**Austlii** (Australasian Legal Information Institute) http://www.austlii.edu.au/austlii for access to Australian legal materials.

**British and Irish Legal Information Institute (BAILII)**
http://www.bailii.org/bailii/. Provides access to British & Irish primary legal materials on the internet.

**Solicitors Online**
http://www.solicitors-online.com. Database of solicitors, based on records from the Law Society of England and Wales.

# Library Catalogues/Subject Bibliographies

The **British Library Public Catalogue** (http:// blpc.bl.uk) is a web interface to the main British Library catalogues. British Library Net also has a number of links to BL WebCats (http:// www.britishlibrary.net/webcats.html). These include the National Sound Archive http:// www.bl.uk/collections/sound-archive/cat.html whose catalogue covers details of almost two-and-a-half million recordings in all genres, from pop, jazz, classical and world music to wildlife sounds, oral history, drama, literature, language and dialect; and the Newspaper Library Catalogue.

**BUBL Journals**
http://bubl.ac.uk/journals/. Provides links to contents, abstracts or full texts of over 200 current journals and newsletters.

**Sirsi Limited**, who sell the Unicorn library management system, have a link to the library catalogues of customers using their WebCat software.

The link is under the heading "WebCat in Europe" on their site at http://www.sirsi.co.uk.

# Maps

### Expedia maps
http://maps.expedia.com. Covers street maps of the United States and road maps of Canada, Mexico and Europe.

### UK street maps
http://www.streetmap.co.uk. Provides address searching and street map facilities for the UK. The site contains street and road maps for the whole of mainland Britain.

# Market research information

### International Market Research Mall
http://www.imrmall.com is a web based community of market research providers.

### Marketresearch.com
http://www.marketresearch.com has details of over 37,000 titles from more than 350 leading publishers.

# Media *see* News & Media

# Medical information *see* Health & medical information

# Museums

### MUSÉE Online Museum Directory
http://www.musee-online.org/. Directory of museums worldwide which can either be searched using criteria such as geographic location or museum type; or the listing can be browsed alphabetically.

# News & Media

### BBC News Search
http://newssearch.bbc.co.uk/ksenglish/query.htm. Contains archive of BBC News Online's stories dating back to November 1997.

### CNET Search.com – news & media
http://www.search.com/search?channel=5&tag=st.se.fd.out.5- Includes coverage of breaking news.

### ft.com
http://www.ft.com. Includes free access to over 10 million newspaper and magazine articles from over 2000 publications; a free guide to key web sites and stories from the Financial Times and ft.com.

### Guardian Unlimited Archive Search
http://www.guardian.co.uk/Archive/0,4271,210474,00.html provides accesss to all Guardian and Observer articles which have appeared on the network from September 1, 1998.

### MediaUK
http://directory.mediauk.com. Covers television, radio, magazines, newspapers and newsfeeds. There is also a "DeepSearch" facility to search around 1800 news web sites.

### Moreover.com
http://www.moreover.com dynamic database providing stories from around 1800 sources. Moreover.com is a search engine focussing on business related web content.

### Northern Light News Alerts
http://standard.northernlight.com/cgi-bin/cl_cliplist.pl. This facility lets users save search profiles. Searches are undertaken across both the contents of Northern Light's web index and their Special Collection (see page 60). If any new items (whether newly published or new to Northern Light's index) match your search criteria, you receive an email alert.

## Patents & Trademarks

### esp@cenet
http://gb.espacenet.com/ is provided by the European Patent Organisation. It is possible to search all the patent applications published in the last two years (or more in some cases) by any national office in the EPO.

### US Trademark Electronic Search System
http://tess.uspto.gov/. Covers more than 2.9 million pending, registered and dead federal trademarks.

### USPTO Web Patent Database
http://www.uspto.gov/patft contains the full text of all US patents issued since 1976 and full-page images of all US patents issued since 1790.

# People

**192.Com**
http://www.192.com

**Biography.com**
http://www.biography.com

**WED World Email Directory**
http://www.worldemail.com/. Contains around 18 million email addresses and more than 140 million business and telephone addresses.

# Poetry

**RhymeZone**
http://rhyme.lycos.com. RhymeZone is an online tool for writers to find words. It can be used to find rhymes, synonyms, anonyms, definitions, homophones, similar sound, same consonants, and related words.

# Postcodes

**Royal Mail's postcodes on-line**
http://www.royalmail.co.uk/paf/. This site covers UK postcodes and you can find an address by searching on a postcode; or a postcode by searching on an address.

# Property

**UpMyStreet.com**
http://www.upmystreet.com has details of UK property prices, nearby schools, council tax, crime

& health statistics local services and stores, and you can also search classified ads.

**Your mortgage**
http://www.propertyprices.co.uk. Includes UK house price projections for the next five years, searchable by postcode and property type.

# Public Records

**familyrecords.gov**
http://www.familyrecords.gov.uk covers information and links about the main UK family history sites on the web including links to external genealogy sites at http://www.familyrecords.gov.uk/linksmain.htm

**Gary Price's Direct Search State/Province and city compilation** of many specialized searchable / interactive databases which covers US/ Canada state/province/city resources. http://gwis2.circ.gwu.edu/~gprice/state.htm

**Public Records Office**
http://www.pro.gov.uk

# Quotations

**xrefer**
http://www.xrefer.com contains encyclopedias, dictionaries, thesauri and books of quotations.

# Ready Reference

**Cambridge Dictionaries Online**
http://dictionary.cambridge.org/ has searchable

dictionaries of English, American English, idiom and phrasal verbs.

**Encarta**
http://www.encarta.msn.com/. Default.asp Encarta is a learning resource with educational content and tools.

**Encyclopedia Britannica**
http://www.britannica.com

**Lexis-Nexis Source Locator**
http://www.lexis-nexis.com/lncc/sources/. The source locator covers an annotated listing of over 31,000 Lexis-Nexis sources.

**Telecom Acronym Reference**
http://www.tiaonline.org/resources/acronym.cfm contains over 2300 acronyms.

# Science

**ResearchIndex**
http://www.researchindex.com/. The NECI scientific literature digital library aims to improve the dissemination and feedback of scientific literature. ResearchIndex provides algorithms, techniques, and software that can be used in other digital libraries. The service indexes Postscript and PDF research articles on the web. It uses Autonomous Citation Indexing (ACI) to autonomously create a citation index that can be used for literature search and evaluation.

## Statistics

**InfoNation**
http://www.un.org/Pubs/CyberSchoolBus/
infonation/e_i_map.htm. This service has up to
date statistical data for the member states of the
United Nations.

## Streaming Media

**Speechbot**
http://speechbot.research.compaq.com/ is a
search engine for audio & video content that is
hosted and played from other websites. It uses
speech recognition to generate transcripts.

## Subject Bibliographies *see* Library
## Catalogues/Subject Bibliographies

## Taxation/Benefits

**Cash or car?**
http://www.cashorcar.co.uk/default.
html?ref–30631881868315404 shows the most tax
efficient way to a "Virtual Company Car". The site
helps users to decide whether to opt for a company
car or a cash alternative.

**Tax calculator**
http://www.i-resign.com/uk/home/default.asp.
The calculator is based on the income tax rates and
allowances and the national insurance rates for the
UK. Users key in their gross yearly income and tick
other appropriate boxes about their circumstances,

and this facility calculates how much of their salary ends up in their pockets.

## Telephone Directories

### BT PhoneNet UK
http://www.bt.com/phonenetuk is a telephone directory covering UK business and residential numbers.

### TelDir.com: telephone directories on the web
http://www.teldir.com/eng contains links to online phone directories for over 170 countries

### Yell
http://www.yell.co.uk is the online version of the UK Yellow Pages of companies classified by subject.

## Timetables

### Cheapflights.com
http://www.cheapflights.com has details of flights and air fares with links to the websites of individual airlines.

### Railtrack – travel information
http://www.railtrack.co.uk/travel

### Teletext
http://www.teletext.co.uk/holidays/flights1.asp?intSubSectionID=28. Information about flights.

# 7. Sample enquiries answered using the invisible web

This chapter illustrates the potential of the invisible web to answer a range of enquiries.

Good web searchers have a thorough knowledge of the search engines with all their limitations; a knowledge of other internet search tools; but above all a knowledge of individual sources, with their strengths and weaknesses. Library and information professionals answering enquiries build up a body of knowledge based on experience. Through their work answering a wide range of enquiries, librarians get to know the best sources and the well respected organisations publishing material on specific topics. When they get an enquiry, they might think immediately of three or four places to check, based on dealing with similar enquiries in the past. And so it is with the internet. If you have a good knowledge of some of the websites, you are more likely to get good results from them rather than going to the search engines. But there are often enquiries that you have which you haven't dealt with before. Using the internet, you might go to your favourite search engine, and if that doesn't come up with the answer, you might then try one or two other search engines. Then you might try a specialist portal site which indexes sites on the topic you have been asked about. If all that fails, then you could try a few of the directories of invisible web sources such as invisibleweb.com or ProFusion.

Another approach would be to establish which organisations are likely to have produced research reports, statistics, or whatever, relating to the topic of your enquiry, locate their website and check out whether they have the answer. Some people do seem to have the attitude that if they can't find it on the web, then it doesn't exist. The problem with that viewpoint is that there is no single search tool that allows you to search the entire resources accessible through the web; and even if such a tool did exist, it must be pointed out that not everything is visible to the search engines. Indeed, not everything is made available on the web, and certainly not for free. Another concern is the accuracy and reliability of material on the web. A survey conducted for Hoover's Online Europe (MORI, 2000) found that few dot.com workers are making vital checks and balances on the business information they obtain via the Internet. The report found that dot.com workers "...are heavily reliant on information obtained from companies' own web sites and appear to be less aware of their shortcomings" (compared with mainstream "not.com" companies).

Information professionals who are good at their job are ones who regard the internet as only one of the tools available to them, albeit one of the most important ones. People should not be ashamed of using the internet in combination with hard copy sources. For example, Aslib publishes the "Aslib directory of information sources in the United Kingdom" (Aslib, 2000a). The index to the publication is very thorough. Indeed, it runs to over 150 pages. Once you have identified organisations that cover topics of interest, the directory gives the URL's of the websites of the organisations. It really depends on the type of enquiry that you get as to which are the best starting points. If you get a statistical enquiry, for example, it might be worth looking at hard copy sources such as the "Guide to official statistics" or "Sources of unofficial UK statistics" (Mort & Wilkins, 2000).

### Question: Where can I get more information about science and technology parks?

With this question, I thought that it would be worth checking Google for PDF documents. I therefore searched for the phrase "science parks" and for the item type PDF by entering the following search statement:

"science parks" inurl:PDF

The first result that came up was:

[PDF] www.britishcouncil.org/science/science/pubs/ukitt/parks.pdf. Essential Sources of Information on Innovation and Technology Transfer 7. Science Parks, Incubators & Spin-Outs 7.1 Introduction The term 'Science Park' is ... Text version - Similar pages

The URL leads to a document "Essential sources of information on innovation and technology transfer. 7. Science parks, incubators & spin-outs" which contains details of literature on the topic, plus a listing of organisations, advisory bodies and UK companies.

Searching by record format rather than purely by subject may seem odd. But there are good reasons why it might be helpful.

- If something has been deemed to be worth capturing in PDF format, it would suggest that someone has decided that the document is particularly useful.

- The kinds of organisations that produce PDF documents are often government departments and agencies.

**Question: What is the percentage of people in the North East of England who own their own home?**

With an enquiry like this I would immediately be thinking about whether there might be any official statistics from the UK government, or data put out by a trade association.

The Office for National Statistics (ONS) website (http://www.statistics.gov.uk) is an excellent site containing a significant amount of data in its own right, as well as links to sources available from other government departments.

There is a listing of the publications that are available online at http://www.statistics.gov.uk/nsbase/OnlineProducts/default.asp. Amongst the titles available is the annual publication Regional Trends. On further examination chapter 6 covers housing, and section 6.4 covers tenure of dwellings under the following headings:

- Owner-occupied.
- Rented from local authority or New Town.

- Rented from private owners or with job or business.
- Rented from registered social landlord.

and the information is broken down by region.

Knowing that the electronic version of "Regional Trends" would be a good place to check for this kind of enquiry is something that comes with experience.

For those who are not so familiar with ONS publications, it is worth doing a text search of Statbase. The problem is really one of selecting the right terminology eg

- Housing.
- Home ownership.
- Tenure of dwellings.

I tried out a number of means of tracking down the right dataset. The phrase "home ownership" retrieved the following:

Socio-economic group of head of household: by tenure, 1998-99: Social Trends Dataset. Traditionally, housing tenure in the United Kingdom has been closely related to social class and economic status. In 1998-99 home ownership was generally more common among those in non-manual groups than those in the manual groups, even though increases in home ownership over the previous 15 years w...

Whereas, searching for the word "Tenure" retrieved http://www.statistics.gov.uk/statbase/xsdataset. asp?vlnk=1421 which is a dataset entitled "National monitor for Great Britain – tenure and amenities selected categories".

Searching on Google did retrieve a discussion thread from the FreePint bar on this topic. But it would not have come up in the first few results with a search on:

"home ownership north east" or
"home owners north east".

It only came up in the top few results with a search on "homeowners north east". The thread that was retrieved is at http://www.freepint.com/bar/read.php?I=6095 in which a user of FreePint asks where they can find recent statistics of how many homeowners there are in the North East. The thread suggested looking at the Office for National Statistics website and also at that of the Council of Mortgage Lenders (CML) (http://www.cml.org.uk). It is possible to search the CML site, and by searching on the phrase "home ownership" I retrieved a number of press releases about home ownership in Scotland and Wales, although nothing about home ownership in North East England; but there was also one entitled *Home ownership in the UK is set to grow, research reveals* CML presse release, Thursday 21st September 2000 which referred to a research report, *Home Ownership, House Purchases and Mortgages: International Comparisons.*

I also looked for other government statistical sources on housing. For example, the Office for National Statistics website is organised into themes. One of the themes was "The Natural & Built Environment". Within each theme there is a set of links to other sites. One of the other sites listed was that of the Department of the Environment, Transport and the Regions. The DETR website http://www.detr.gov.uk has a heading for "Housing and housing policy" and within that there is a heading for "Statistics on housing". This led to a link for "Housing statistics 2000" and then to chapter 1.4: Stock of dwellings: By Government Office Regions and tenure (xls file - 55kb)

The open.gov.uk web site is a first entry point to UK public sector information on the internet. There is an alphabetical listing of the main topics for which government bodies produce information for the internet at http://www.open.gov.uk/index/topicindex.htm and a heading for "housing" at http://www.open.gov.uk/index/t_housing.htm

### Question: What are the most popular travel destinations for UK holiday makers

The first place that I searched was the Researcha free reports database. Researcha (http://www.researcha.com) is a virtual community of information professionals. The site was launched in October 2000 and since February 2001 the free reports database has been a chargeable part of the service. For £80 + VAT a year users can search the free reports database which has links to useful research reports that are available on the web free of charge. Many of the items covered are not easy to locate on the web. In some cases for example they are only available after completing a registration process.

Searching for holiday or holidays I entered the search statement: holiday* and it retrieved one item:

*Facts and figures on the Europeans on holiday*

http://www.europa.eu.int/comm/enterprise/services/topublications/documents/eubarholi0398.pdf Where the Europeans go for their holiday, how they travel there, stay there, where they book them.

(see page 64 for fuller information on Researcha).

I did also have a look at the Office for National Statistics website to see whether they had any information on the topic. I went to the section for ONS press releases and searched for the word "travel" within the title, and this led me to a press release of 23 November 2000 entitled: "Travel trends: international passenger survey 1999" which showed that the most popular destinations for UK residents in 1999 were:

France, Spain, Irish Republic, USA and Greece.

**What has the UK government been doing about museums in the past 3 months?**

This is quite a difficult question to answer using the search engines. For one thing, whilst you can search for records about museums, it is not quite so easy to filter out those records that do not relate to the UK situation. Some search engines let you search only for records of a certain domain eg. records ending in .uk But that would exclude any UK sites which are .com or .net sites, for example.

I had a look on Northern Light using the search statement: museums government policy uk.

This retrieved 66,028 records, and the first items retrieved were:

1.     Culture in the UK – outline of government structure and responsibilities..

2.     Usage statistics for epaa.asu.edu.

3.     Heritage, libraries & museums press releases Mar-Jan 00.

4.     House of Commons – Culture Media and Sport – Minutes of Evidence.

5.     Press release ….MGC advocates new approach for rural museums.

I went back and tried a more precise search using the Power Search facility on Northern Light at http://www.northernlight.com/power.html and this time limited the search to government web sites within the required date range (since the beginning of 2001), where the sites were from the United Kingdom. This retrieved 167 items in 64 sources. Whilst some of the results retrieved would have had some useful information in them, it would have required quite a bit of time to wade through the sites to pick out information that might be useful for this enquiry. So I then moved on to some of the invisible web sites.

Invisible web sources are often better than using the search engines, so long as you can identify appropriate sites to search; because many invisible web sites cover specialist subject areas. So, if you find a site covering the right topic, you are far less likely to retrieve false hits.

With a question like this, what I would do would be to search official material:

- what recent press releases have been issued by government departments on the subject of museums? Using the Central Office of Information press release site at http://www.nds.coi.gov.uk/ it is possible to do a text search within a specific date range, and if required – the search can be restricted to one government department. One press release that was retrieved was headed "Budget 2000" and on examination it said: 'Final obstacle to universal free admission to national museums and galleries is now removed....Culture Secretary Chris Smith today welcomed the news that Britain's national museums and galleries will shortly be able to scrap all remaining admission charges, thanks to Budget changes, announced by the Chancellor'.

- have there been any questions in parliament? Were these as parliamentary questions or as written answers given in Hansard? It is possible to search parliamentary material on the UK parliament pages at http://www.parliament.the-stationery-office.co.uk/cgi-bin/empower?DB=ukparl. One of the records that I retrieved, for example, covered the question of the lending policies of our national museums and galleries:

**26 Feb 2001 : Column 571 Mrs. Ann Cryer (Keighley):** As the national museums and galleries are unable to display their entire collections, does my right hon. Friend agree that, instead of lending out items to private organisations, it would be fairer and better if they followed the example of the science museum, which has links with the national railway museum, York and the national museum of photography, film and television in Bradford? Both those museums are extremely popular and enable people from the north to see those wonderful collections.

• has anyone said anything in parliament about museums in recent debates? http://www.parliamentlive.tv Gordon Brown's budget speech on March 7th saying that "...The government's policy is for free museums, and I can announce that we will change the law on VAT to make that possible".

I did try and look for suitable sites using some of the directories of invisible web resources such as Complete Planet. However, I tend to find that as these are just directory listings rather than full text search engines, that you usually have to do a very rough and ready search that is too broad for your needs, and that you are far better off going directly to the best sites for the topic. The problem, of course, is knowing what those sites are. I have built up a knowledge of useful sites over a number of years through having to do a lot of web based enquiry work, but also through tips I have picked up from colleagues at professional events, through reading the professional literature, and also through participating in a number of discussion lists.

# 8. Conclusion

The phrase "the invisible web" is something of a misnomer. The very phrase "the invisible web" conjures up images of a rather secretive underworld. In fact, the invisible web actually consists of open source material – so long as you know how to find it, you are able to access the resources of the invisible web. Indeed, the BrightPlanet white paper (BrightPlanet, 2000) says that a full 95% of the deep web is publicly accessible information – not subject to fees or subscriptions. So, its not a case of hacking or gaining access to material that you are not meant to see.

Invisible web resources can be retrieved "via" the web rather than strictly speaking being "on" the web. The question is how you find them; knowing where they are located. The content of the invisible web is not "invisible", even if it is well hidden. And as people become more and more aware of invisible web resources, they are likely to create hyperlinks to those resources in their – often static – web pages. The invisible web will, therefore, become much more visible. But that still doesn't make it possible to search the entire web in a single search where the complete contents of both the open web and the invisible web are searched in their entirety.

There is undoubtedly a problem. We must above all raise awareness of the problem because hopefully it will mean that webmasters reduce the likelihood of websites being created that are not fully searchable; and, hopefully, it will lead information professionals to become familiar with directories and indices of invisible web resources and perhaps also with a selection of some of the most useful resources in their own right.

I am sure that the search engines will do everything they can to find a technical solution to the problem of the invisible web. Google in particular seems to have already undertaken a number of major initiatives such as the indexing of PDF documents, or the purchase of the Deja newsgroup archive. But the reality is that individual search engines do not cover the whole of the visible web, let alone the invisible web. So the prospect of there being a single search engine which has complete coverage of the entire web is some way off.

The internet is the subject of rapid and relentless change. The search engines are constantly trying to increase their coverage of the web; and to improve their functionality. Information professionals therefore need to work extremely hard to keep up to date with developments in order to ensure that they are up to speed on which are the best search engines, whether in terms of the extent of their coverage; their functionality; or, in the case of specialist search engines which limit themselves to resources pertinent to their subject specialism, the quality of the sites they list. Sites change, and what was a good site a few months ago may no longer have the very things on it that made it so good previously. In order to keep abreast of developments I would particularly recommend the internet discus-

sion lists of the FreePint bar (http://
www.freepint.com/bar) and also BUSLIB-L business librarians discussion list (http://
listserv.boistestate.edu/archives/buslib-L.html);
ResearchBuzz (http://www.researchbuzz.com)
which covers the field of internet research; Danny
Sullivan's Search Engine Watch (http://
www.searchenginewatch.com) and Greg Notess's
Search Engine Showdown (http://www.
searchengineshowdown.com).

Then there is peer to peer computing which will
have a dramatic effect on the capacity of individu-
als to find real nuggets of information because they
are searching thousands of hard drives of internet
searchers, rather than a centralised web server. Up
to now it has been primarily used to search for and
or swap music tracks. But it has infinitely greater
potential than that. Services such as Gnutella and
Pointera are making use of peer to peer computing.

During the preparation of this book I found that
no sooner had I viewed a number of websites and
subsequently written some notes about them, then
suddenly those very same websites had changed.
Perhaps their index had now increased its coverage of invisible web resources, or – as in the case of
Google – you were now able to search PDF documents which were previously not covered by any
of the mainstream search engines. The internet is a
moving target. It is getting bigger all the time. However, unless search engines reach the point where
they are able to index the entire contents of the web
– both those of the visible web and what we currently refer to as the "invisible web" – at least once

a day, then we are always going to have an "invisible web". There are plenty of sites that are constantly updated throughout the day such as streaming media, news and current affairs sites. Unless the search engines are able to cope with the speed of updating for sites like that, then there is bound to be a time lag of weeks or indeed months before many items get to be indexed on the search engines.

# 9. References and further reading

Abreu, Elinor (2000). Diving into the deep web *The Standard*, September 4. http://www.thestandard.com/article/display/0,1151,18134,00.html

American University Library (2000). *Links to the "invisible web"*... and what exactly does that term mean? http://www.library.american.edu/invisibleweb.html

Aslib (2000a). Aslib directory of information sources in the United Kingdom edited by Keith W Reynard, 11th ed. ISBN 0851424309.

Aslib (2000b). *Managing Information*, November, 20.

Associated Press (2000). Search technologies explore "invisible web" *USA Today Tech Report*, 27th July. http://www.usatoday.com/life/cyber/tech/cti290.htm

Barker, Joe (2001). Seeing the invisible web. University of California, Berkeley Libraries. http://lib.berkeley.edu/TeachingLib/Guides/Internet/InvWebPowerpoint/index.htm

Basch, R. & Bates, M. (2000). Researching online for dummies. IDG Books. ISBN 0764505467.

Bates, Mary Ellen (2001). The use of the internet in special librarianship in Handbook of information management edited by Alison Scammell. London: Aslib. ISBN 0851424570.

Benjamin, Kay (2000a). Discovering the invisible web. Presented September 29, for South Central Regional Library Council. http://www.oneonta. edu/~libweb/kb/invisiblescrlc.html

Benjamin, Kay (2000b). The invisible web. Oneonta University Library, April 6. http://www.oneonta. edu/~libweb/kb/invisibleweb.html

Blakeman, K. (2001). Tales from the Terminal Room No 17 http://www.rba.co.uk/tfttr/index.htm

Botluk, Diana (1999). Exposing the invisible web. Law Library Resource Xchange, October 1. http://www.llrx.com/columns/exposing.htm

Botluk, Diana (2000). Mining deeper into the invisible web. Law Library Resource Xchange (LLRX), November 15. http://www.llrx.com/features/mining.htm

BrightPlanet (2000). The deep web: surfacing hidden value. White paper. BrightPlanet, July. 41pp. http://www.completeplanet.com/Tutorials/DeepWeb/index.asp

Bruemmer, P. (2000). Using doorway pages to register. ASP web sites. *Clickz Network*, 27th September. http://www.clickz.com/cgi-bin/gt/article.html?article=2489

Charny, B (2000). The world wide $#@%@$ing web! December 23. http://www.zdnet.com/zdnn/stories/news/0,4586,2667216,00.html

Coursey, David (2001). I can search the "invisible web". Here's how you can too. *ZDNet*, February 8. http://www.zdnet.com/anchordesk/stories/story/0,10738,2683349,00.html

Cyveillance (2000). Internet exceeds 2 billion pages. *Press release*, 10th July. http://cyveillance.com/newsroom/pressr/000710.asp

Dahn, Michael (2000a). Counting angels on a pinhead: critically interpreting web size estimates. *Online* 24 No 1, January. http://www.onlineinc.com/onlinemag/OL2000/dahn1.html

Dahn, Michael (2000b). Spotlight on the invisible web. *Online*, July Vol 24, No 4. http://www.findarticles.com/m1388/4_24/63568434/p1/article.jhtml

Dupont (1999). Legal deposit in Denmark – the new law and electronic products. *LIBER Quarterly: the journal of European research libraries* Vol 9, No 2 http://www.kb.nl/infolev/liber/articles/dupont11.htm

Google (2001). Google acquires usenet discussion service and significant assets from Deja.com. *Google press release*, February 12th. http://groups.google.com/intl/en_extra/press/pressrel/pressrelease48.html

Guernsey, Lisa (2001). Mining the "Deep Web" with specialized drills. New York Times, January 25. http://www.nytimes.com/2001/01/25/technology/25SEAR.html

Harris, Robert (2001). World wide web research tools: fortunately the haystack is indexed. Vanguard

University of Southern California, February 15. http://vanguard.edu/rharris/search.htm

Hartman, Karen and Ackermann, Ernest (2000). The invisible web: a presentation at Computers in Libraries 2000. http://www.webliminal.com/essentialweb/invisible.html

Inkrote, Joelle (1999). Internet tips: searching the invisible web, November 29. http://www.amigos.org/aaoc/1999/nov99/tips.html

Inktomi (2000). Web surpasses one billion documents. *Press release*, 18th January. http://www.inktomi.com/new/press/2000/billion.html

Kent State University Libraries & Media (2000). *Searching the invisible web*. http://www.library.kent.edu/internet/invisible_web/

Lawrence, Steve and Giles, C. Lee (1999). Accessibility of information on the web *Nature 400*, No. 6740, July 8, 107-109. (See also a summary of the study at http://www.wwwmetrics.com).

Maclay, K. (2000). UC Berkeley professors measure exploding world production of new information. *University of California, Berkeley press release* 18th October, 2000. http://www.berkeley.edu/news/media/releases/2000/10/18_info.html reporting the findings of the report "How much information" by Hal Varian and Peter Lyman which can be accessed at http://www.sims.berkeley,edu/how-much-info/index.html

McCarthy, Shawn P (1999). The search is on for ways to navigate invisible web sites. *Government*

*Computers News* February 22. http://www.gcn.com/archives/gcn/1999/February22/37b.htm

McDonnell, Matthew (2001). Presentation at the City Information Group meeting on Making the web visible, February. http://www.cityinfogroup.co.uk/Downloads.shtml

Mickey, Bill (2000). When is a billion too much? *ONLINE*, September. http://www.onlineinc.com/onlinemag/OL2000/editorial9.html

MORI (2000). Dot.comers rely on "dubious" business information. Mori polls archive, 15 December. http://www.mori.com/polls/2000/hoovers.htm

Mort, D. and Wilkins, W. (2000). Sources of unofficial UK statistics 4th ed. Aldershot, Gower ISBN 0566082365. 2000.

Notess, Greg R (1997). On the net: searching the hidden internet. *Database* 20 No 3, June. http://www.onlineinc.com/database/JunDB97/nets6.html

O'Leary, Mick (2000). Invisible web discovers hidden treasures. *Information Today*, January, Vol 17 No 1, 16-18.

Office of National Statistics (2000). Guide to official statistics. London: The Stationery Office. ISBN 011621161X.

Pedley, Paul (2000). The invisible web. *Library Association Record*, November, Vol 102 No 11, 628, 633. http://www.la-hq.org.uk/directory/record/r200011/article2.html

Pedley, Paul (2001). Searching the invisible web. In *Forum*, March-April. Databeuro.

Price, Gary and Sherman, Chris (2000a). Around the world in 80 sites: the best of the invisible web presented at Online World 2000, September 16. http://websearch.about.com/internet/websearch/library/blow2000.htm

Price, Gary and Sherman, Chris (2000b). The invisible web. Presentation at Internet Librarian 2000, November 5-9, Monterey CA. http://www.infotoday.com/il2000/presentations/sherman1.ppt http://gwu.edu/~gprice/invisiblewebexamples.htm (URL's from Gary & Chris's presentation)

Price, Gary and Sherman, Chris (2001). The invisible web: uncovering information sources search engines can't see. CyberAge Books. ISBN: 091096551X.

Re: source (2000). British Library "urgently" needs legal deposit powers for electronic materials – Resource responds to culture department review of British Library. *Re: source press release*, 18 December. http://www.resource.gov.uk/news/pr2000_26.html

Roger Williams University Library (2000). The invisible web: search tools and subject directories. University Library. September 13. http://library.rwu.edu/invisible.html

Roll, Donald (2001). Presentation at the City Information Group meeting on Making the web visible, February. http://www.cityinfogroup.co.uk/Downloads.shtml

Sherman, Chris (1999a). The invisible web. *About.com*. http://websearch.about.com/internet/websearch/library/weekly/aa061199.htm

Sherman, Chris (1999b). Search bots and agents. *About.com*. http://websearch.about.com/internet/websearch/library/weekly/aa022699.htm

Sherman, Chris (2000a). The almost visible web. *About.com*. http://websearch.about.com/internet/websearch/library/weekly/aa091800a.htm

Sherman, Chris (2000b). The invisible web. *FreePint* No 64 (Feature article), 8 June. http://www.freepint.co.uk/issues/080600.htm#feature

Sherman, Chris (2000c). Tooling around the invisible web. *About.com*. http://websearch.about.com/internet/websearch/library/weekly/aa061300a.htm

Sherman, Chris (2000d). The web less travelled. *About.com*. http://websearch.about.com/internet/library/weekly/aa011800a.htm

Sherman, C. (2001a). What's ahead for 2001?: predictions from 13 information industry sages. *Information Today*, Issue 1, January. http://www.infotoday.com/it/jan01/whatsahead.htm).

Sherman, Chris (2001b). Google ventures into the invisible web: the web's first large-scale PDF search. *About.com*. http://websearch.about.com/internet/websearch/library/weekly/aa013101a.htm

Sherman, Chris (2001c). Invisible web – hidden searchable sites http://websearch.about.com/internet/websearch/cs/invisibleweb1/

Sherman, Chris (2001d). Invisible web gateways http://websearch.about.com/internet/websearch/msub12-m30.htm

Sherman, Chris (2001e). Invisible web databases – searchable databases on the web http://websearch.about.com/internet/websearch/msub12-m31.htm

Smith, Ian (2001). The invisible web: where search engines fear to go http://www.powerhomebiz.com/vol25/invisible.htm

Snow, Bonnie (2000). The internet's hidden content and how to find it. *Online*, May, Vol 24, No 3, 61-66

Sullivan, Danny (1999). "Invisible web" revealed. *The Search Engine Report*, July 6. http://www.searchenginewatch.com/sereport/99/07-invisible.html

Sullivan, Danny (2000a). Invisible web gets deeper. *The Search Engine Report*, August 2. http://www.searchenginewatch.com/sereport/00/08-deepweb.html

Sullivan, Danny (2000b). Specialty search engines ... Invisible web. http://www.searchenginewatch.com/links/Specialty_Search_Engines/Invisible_Web/index.html

Sullivan, Danny (2001). Google does PDF & other changes. *The Search Engine Report*, February 6. http://searchenginewatch.com/sereport/01/02-google.html

University of California, Berkeley. Library (2000). Beyond general world wide web searching (Teaching library internet workshops). September 21. http:/ /www.lib.berkeley.edu/TeachingLib/Guides/ Internet/BeyondWeb.html

University of California, Berkeley. Library (2001). The invisible web: database contents rarely found in search engines. (Teaching library internet workshops). http:/ /www.lib.berkeley.edu/TeachingLib/ Guides/Internet/InvisibleWeb.html

University of Chicago at Illinois (2000). Reclaiming the internet's original purpose. *UIC news tips*. 17th August.

Vidmar, Dale (2000). Internet searching tools. Southern Oregon University. http:/ /www.sou. edu/library/cybrary/search.htm

Warnick, Walter L (2001). Searching the deep web: directed query engine applications at the Department of Energy. *D-Lib Magazine*, January. Vol 7 No 1. http://www.dlib.org/dlib/january01/warnick/ 01warnick.html

Wiseman, Ken (1999). The invisible web: searching the hidden parts of the internet. Fall. http:// www.apple.com/education/LTReview/fall99/ invisibleweb/ and http://www3.dist214.k12.il.us/ invisible/article/invisiblearticle.html

# Glossary

## Doorway pages

Where companies modify pages for the purpose of search engine optimisation these are known as "doorway pages", "gateway pages" or "splash pages".

## MP3

the most common format for transferring music files over the web.

## Spider

A spider is a program that automatically visits and reads web pages in order to create an entry in a search engine index. Spiders are so called because they crawl across the web. Another term that is sometimes used is webcrawler.

## Streaming media

Streaming media is content that contains audio, video and other media types.

## Z39.50

National Information Standards Organization Z39.50 Information Retrieval Protocol (Z39.50/ISO 23950 defines a standard way for two computers to communicate for the purpose of information retrieval.

# Index

# Aslib Know How Guides

*Assessing Information Needs: Tools, Techniques and Concepts for the Internet Age (2nd ed)*

*Copyright for Library and Information Service Professionals (2nd ed)*

*Developing a Records Management Programme*

*Disaster Planning for Library and Information Services*

*Effective Financial Planning for Library and Information Services*

*Email for Library and Information Professionals (2nd ed)*

*Evaluation of Library and Information Services (2nd ed)*

*How to Market Your Library Service Effectively (2nd ed)*

*How to Promote Your Web Site Effectively*

*Information Resources Selection*

*The Internet for Library and Information Service Professionals (3rd ed)*

*Intranets and Push Technology: Creating an Information-Sharing Environment*

*Job Descriptions for the Information Profession*

*Knowledge Management: Linchpin of Change*

*Legal Information – What It Is and Where to Find It (2nd ed)*

*Legal Liability for Information Provision*

*Making a Charge for Library and Information Services*

*Managing Change in Libraries and Information Services*

*Managing Film and Video Collections*

*Managing Library Automation*

*Moving Your Library*

*Performance Measurement in Library and Information Services*

*Preparing a Guide to Your Library and Information Service*

*Project Management for Library and Information Service Professionals*

*Researching for Business: Avoiding the 'Nice to Know' Trap*

*Strategic Planning for Library and Information Services*

*Teleworking for Library and Information Professionals*

*World Wide Web: How to Design and Construct Web Pages (2nd ed)*